Sea Girt

NEW JERSEY

Sea Girt

NEW JERSEY

A BRIEF HISTORY

Joseph G. Bilby

THE History PRESS

Published by The History Press
Charleston, SC 29403
www.historypress.net

Cover design by Marshall Hudson.

First published 2008
Second printing 2008

Manufactured in the United States

ISBN 978.1.59629.449.3

Library of Congress Cataloging-in-Publication Data

Bilby, Joseph G.
Sea Girt, New Jersey : a brief history / Joseph G. Bilby.
p. cm.
ISBN 978-1-59629-449-3
1. Sea Girt (N.J.)--History. I. Title.
F144.S4B55 2008
974.9'46--dc22
2008019186

This book is dedicated to the professional and volunteer staff whose hard work, technical skills and support make the National Guard Militia Museum of New Jersey in Sea Girt everything it is.

Contents

Preface

At first glance, the tale of a quiet little New Jersey seacoast town encompassing but a square mile of land that did not become a municipality until 1917, had virtually no population prior to 1875 and fewer than six hundred permanent residents as late as 1940 might not seem to hold a lot of potential, much less the material for a book. But a second, more serious glance, penetrating the haze of history that has closed over the borough of Sea Girt for the past several generations, reveals that the town played a role in a series of significant but forgotten events in the narrative of New Jersey and the nation. That fascinating story unfolded for me as I wrote this book, and I hope it will prove equally absorbing for the reader.

Acknowledgements

No work of this kind is produced in a vacuum, and I owe a lot of people thanks for their inspiration, advice, research assistance, encouragement and constructive criticism. Rather than even begin to try to break down the details of the generosity of those who have helped, and with the possibility of missing some deserving soul, I have decided to list them in alphabetical order: Peter Anderson, Joseph M. Boa, Barbara Borab, Frances Brown, Fred Burns, Lieutenant Colonel (retired) and Sea Girt Mayor Marc Clemmensen, Sea Girt Lighthouse Trustee Bill Dunn, Rick Erickson, Sea Girt Councilman Ken Farrell, NGMMNJ Curator First Lieutenant Jarrett Feldman, NGMMNJ Assistant Curator Carol Fowler, Monmouth County Historical Commission Executive Director Randy Gabrielan, Steve Garratano, Jack and Betty Geiger, Jack Hendrickson, Samuel Kaye, Monmouth County Archives Research Assistant Mary Ann Kiernan, Jim Madden, Joshua Mamaclay, C.V. "Bud" Norris, National Guard Training Center Director Brigadier General (retired) Jeffrey Pierson, Sea Girt Librarian Anne Ryan, Jerry Travers, Richard O. Venino, Esq., and Harry Ziegler—oh, and slightly out of order, but always hovering about in spirit and inspiration, Governor A. Harry Moore, wherever you are. Needless to say, any omissions or errors in this work are my fault alone.

CHAPTER 1

Lenape to Salt Makers

Along the New Jersey Shore, as everywhere else in New Jersey, in the beginning there were the Native Americans, the Leni-Lenape. The Lenape then living in today's Monmouth County, like other New Jersey Indians, moved their camps with the seasons. A long-held belief that few Lenape ever lived in the area, but that Indians from far inland came "down the shore" to harvest fish and shellfish on a seasonal basis, has been disputed in recent years, and relics found in the county are now viewed as evidence of a permanent population. The majority of resident Native Americans lived in the northern part of the county, however, with a population center near the current town of Red Bank. There is no substantive archaeological evidence of Native American presence in the actual stretch of oceanfront land that includes modern Sea Girt. A recent study of the 171 acres included in the New Jersey National Guard Training Center located in the southern section of the town reported that "no prehistoric artifacts were recovered and no archeological sites were identified." Despite this, there is no doubt that Lenape traveled in the general area of Sea Girt during at least part of the year. An early archaeological survey revealed discoveries indicating a possible village site a few miles north, near the Shark River Inlet at Belmar, and found "scattered specimens [of stone tools and implements] on the point of land at nearby Brielle and Manasquan." The survey also noted that "scattered relics are found on the points of land between Manasquan and the ocean front" along the Manasquan River, and others in Point Pleasant Borough to the south, indicating that area was probably home to a resident Indian population of undetermined size. Anecdotal evidence of projectile point discoveries near Wreck Pond, located at the northern border of Sea Girt, suggests it may have been a location visited by Native American fishermen as well.[1]

Before the coming of Europeans, the people of New Jersey, inhabitants of the homeland of *Lenapehoking*, a territory covering portions of several modern states, were members of the Minsi (north) and Unami (central and south) language subgroups. Along with growing corn, beans and squash, the Lenape also hunted game, including white-tailed deer, birds and small mammals; gathered nuts and berries; and fished in inlets, bays and rivers. Shellfish were eaten fresh or dried. They were also a source of tools made from shells, and, in the case of clamshells, the components of a money-like product called wampum, as well as jewelry. Middens, or large piles of oyster shells, have been discovered at many sites along the New Jersey coast, from Raritan Bay to Cape May, and survived as evidence of industrious Lenape shell fishermen for many years, until European colonists and their descendants began to use them as construction and road paving material. Other middens were buried during twentieth-century construction projects.[2]

The first European to sail the New Jersey coast was Giovanni de Verrazano, an Italian employed by King Francis I of France. In the spring of 1524, as the Lenape along the shore watched Verrazano's ship glide by on its way northward, it is doubtful they anticipated what was in store for them and their descendants over the next two centuries. One thing that can be said, though, is that they were not afraid. When Verrazano's ship rounded Sandy Hook into Raritan Bay, large numbers of Indians rushed down to the shore with great excitement, launching canoes to get a closer look at the white men. Prevailing winds prevented a landing, however, postponing a face-to-face meeting between Lenape and Europeans. There is no existing evidence of any closer encounters for the rest of the sixteenth century, although one or more are certainly possible, considering that a number of European fishermen and explorers sailed into American waters over those years.[3]

The next verifiable contact between the Lenape and Europeans in what is now coastal Monmouth County occurred when Henry Hudson, an Englishman exploring on behalf of the Dutch, entered Raritan Bay in 1609. As in 1524, the Indians demonstrated no fear of their visitors, but on this occasion what began as seemingly innocuous trading opportunities ended badly. The cultural insensitivity, bullying and outright theft Hudson's men displayed during a number of forays into Raritan and New York Bays resulted in several deadly incidents, including one in which a sailor was killed by a flint-tipped arrow in the throat, and another in which eight or ten Lenape were blown out of the water and several canoes were sunk by small arms and cannon fire from Hudson's ship, the *Half Moon*.[4]

Dutch traders followed in Hudson's wake and their voyages produced more detailed maps of the Raritan Bay coast. The directors of the Dutch West India Company staked a claim to the mid-Atlantic area of North America, which they named New Netherland. The company was more interested in establishing posts to trade for furs, rather than establishing permanent populations of colonists, as were the English to the north and south. New Netherland, always thinly populated, extended at one time or another over parts of the current states of Connecticut, New York, New Jersey, Pennsylvania, Delaware and Maryland. The first West India Company presence in the modern state of New Jersey was limited to fur trading stations along the lower Delaware River, where the Dutch came into contact with English and Swedish traders on the same mission. Outposts established as part of these mercantile efforts in 1624 were subsequently abandoned and then rebuilt in the 1630s.[5]

Settlements farther north, on Manhattan Island and at Fort Orange (Albany), were more enduring. As the Dutch occupation of New Netherland began to assume a degree of permanence, especially in the environs of Manhattan, the West India Company established settlements to supply the colony with locally produced food. To this end the

The Lenape lived off the land by fishing, hunting, gathering and agriculture. *Courtesy Monmouth County Historical Commission.*

company awarded patroonships, or land grants, to wealthy merchants who guaranteed to establish large farming estates along the North (Hudson) River. Patroon Michiel Reyniersz Pauw received such a grant across the river from New Amsterdam in 1630. Pauw's agent, Cornelius Van Vorst, established the first farm or "bouwerie," Pavonia, within the boundaries of modern Jersey City.[6]

Few settlers followed Van Vorst, and Pavonia reverted to the West India Company, which rented some land to commuting New Amsterdamers and leased bouweries to permanent settlers who moved across the river to combine farming with fur trading. The community grew slowly until Governor William Kieft attacked a peaceful Indian village and ignited a bloody Indian war. Most of the Dutch settlers in Pavonia were killed or fled to New Amsterdam, leaving New Netherland only a tiny toehold on the west bank of the North River. The war spread rapidly across New Netherland. Aert Theunisen, trading along the Navesink River, was killed by local Lenape seeking revenge for the massacre of their brothers to the north. Kieft was replaced by the more efficient Peter Stuyvesant in 1647 and Dutch settlements in the area of modern Hudson County slowly began to expand again, with new communities established at Communipaw and Paulus Hook. Another Indian war broke out while Stuyvesant was off subduing Swedish settlements on the Delaware in 1655, however, and most of the Dutch were swept back across the river again, leaving all of their villages and bouweries in ashes, save Communipaw. Subsequent reoccupation of the west shore was more carefully controlled. Following an Indian treaty in 1658, new and returning settlers were formally licensed, ordered to build fortified villages and required to have at least one man capable of bearing arms in each farmstead. The first new village established was Bergen, and it was there to stay.[7]

Unlike Bergen, Dutch North America soon became a thing of the past. The English Civil War and its aftermath, including the execution of King Charles I and the subsequent dictatorship of Oliver Cromwell, ended with the coronation of Charles's son as King Charles II in 1660. In 1664, Charles granted New Netherland to his brother James, Duke of York, based on the premise that John Cabot, a Venetian explorer working for England, had sailed nearby in 1498. Since the Dutch were not likely to agree with the king's award, the duke dispatched a fleet to New Amsterdam to enforce his will. Despite the belligerence of Stuyvesant, who wanted to fight, New Amsterdam, its defenses against a European invader in shambles, quickly capitulated to the British under James's Governor Colonel Richard Nicolls and became New York. Although he recognized existing Dutch settlements, Nicolls wasted no time granting land in the territory across the North River to Englishmen. In April 1665, Nicolls, acting in the duke's name, awarded the Navesink patent to a group of Long Island Quakers and Baptists. Navesink, which gained its name from the Lenape living there, was a roughly triangle-shaped parcel. Its base stretched from Sandy Hook to the mouth of the Raritan River, then twenty-five miles up the Raritan. The border then angled roughly southeast to Barnegat Bay, and back up the coast to Sandy Hook, including present-day Sea Girt within its boundaries. The grantees agreed to settle one hundred families on the land and erect fortifications for their defense.[8]

Nicolls stressed that his land grant, which became the townships of Middletown and Shrewsbury, had to be purchased from the local Lenape. In fact, the new governor was doing no more than validating a March 1664 agreement between the Long Islanders and Navesink chief Popamora. Payment included wampum, shirts, coats, guns, tobacco, wine, gunpowder and lead. Although some local Navesink apparently moved inland after the deal, one account notes that at the time of the purchase "few Indians were permanent residents of the actual shore and its immediately contiguous area." As noted above, this was not necessarily the case, although European-borne disease could well have reduced the local population significantly between 1524 and 1664. At least some Lenape remained in close contact with the settlers for a period of time. A decade later, Richard Hartshorne of Middletown wrote that one could "buy as much of Fish from an *Indian* for half a pound of [gun] Powder as will serve 6 or 8 men; deer are also very plenty in this Province; we can buy a fat buck of the *Indians* much bigger than the *English* deer for a pound and a half of Powder or Lead." A few Navesink were still hunting game and trapping fur bearers to sell to white settlers in Monmouth County as late as 1715.[9]

The Navesink Lenape had traded with the Dutch and English for a number of years, and some New Amsterdam merchants negotiated with local chiefs in hopes of planting a settlement, but no European settlers moved to the area until the advent of the Long Islanders in 1665. Indian understanding of land sales and their believed rights to hunt and fish conflicted with the new inhabitants' European concept of property ownership, however, and led to problems. Angered and confused at being shut out of much of their traditional hunting territory, some Indians began to kill domestic stock and appropriate other material goods. Hartshorne, annoyed by Lenape hunting, fishing, foraging and cutting trees for dugout canoes on Sandy Hook, which he believed he now owned in the English sense, eventually purchased final rights from them, specifying that henceforth "no Indian or Indians, shall or hath no pretense to lands or timber or liberty, privileges on no pretense whatsoever" on his property.[10]

It is unclear how large New Jersey's Native American population actually was at the time of European settlement. Estimates range all over the lot, from 2,400 to 7,000 or 12,000 to a high of 50,000; those tending toward the lower end seem more probable. Whatever the number was, it would never get higher. One estimate is that by 1700 "probably less than six thousand" Indians remained, while another posits that there were only 1,500 Lenape in the colony as early as 1669, with 500 of those living within the boundaries of modern Monmouth County. In contrast, estimates of the white population of East and West Jersey in that period range from 16,000 to 20,000. In the first four decades of the eighteenth century the wobbly Lenape nation, inundated by English settlers, collapsed dramatically. Casualties suffered in Keift's war were vastly exceeded by deadly European-borne epidemics, most notably smallpox, but also including measles and influenza, which periodically swept through the Lenape people and, by one estimate, killed half of them.[11]

In addition to suffering from decimating diseases, New Jersey's Native Americans also were increasingly elbowed aside and confined to a steadily shrinking homeland by a continuing wave of settlement. There seemed no place in the rapidly evolving social and land tenure structure for the time-honored lifestyles of the surviving Lenape. Some Indians attempted to cling to their old customs, while others tried to assimilate to a rapidly changing world, but all became dependent on trade goods, from iron tools and guns to cooking pots, blankets and clothing. Even before 1700, Lenape traditional culture began a rapid decline. One small Unami band living near Trenton "eked out a mendicant existence on the shabby fringes of the white settlements, simultaneously dependent on and resentful of the whites." As the eighteenth century progressed, many Lenape, anxious to preserve what remained of their identity, migrated west of the Delaware River. A 1758 conference at Crosswicks between Indians remaining in the colony and provincial authorities resulted in a buyout of any remaining Lenape claims. Among the ownership issues resolved in 1758 were those of "Tom Store and Andrew Wooley," who "claimed the land from the mouth of Sqan River to the mouth of the Shrewsbury." If this is correct, they were the last Native Americans with claims on today's Sea Girt.[12]

By 1759 there were an estimated 300 Christian Lenape still living in New Jersey, 200 of them on the colony's Indian reservation at Brotherton (today's Indian Mills), a

The Lenape had largely evacuated Monmouth County by 1700. *Courtesy Monmouth County Historical Commission.*

three-thousand-acre tract in Burlington County. One source cites a total of only 200 living on the state's entire coastal plain by 1775. The remaining Brotherton Indians, fewer than 100 in number, left for New Stockbridge in New York in 1801, effectively ending the Lenape presence in the state, although scattered individuals and small family groups apparently remained here and there, primarily in the southern counties. In 1832 the New Jersey Legislature paid $2,000 to 40 Lenape then living with the Stockbridge Indians near Green Bay, Wisconsin, in a final settlement for "the right of fishing in all the rivers and bays south of the Raritan and of hunting in all uninclosed [*sic*] lands." In 1970 there were 4,706 Native Americans residing in the state, 375 of them in Monmouth County; none counted as full-blooded Lenape. Today, although some Native American individuals and groups in New Jersey claim a long-term history in the state, these claims have been disputed. Most modern Lenape live in Oklahoma.[13]

If the Leni-Lenape no longer owned New Jersey, neither, in a sense, did Colonel Nicolls's grantees. Unknown to Nicolls, parceling out property from New York, the Duke of York had transferred land rights beyond the North River to two of his courtiers, Lord John Berkeley and Sir George Carteret. The new proprietors dispatched Sir George's twenty-six-year-old distant cousin Philip Carteret as governor. Along with a new governor, the colony, initially dubbed Albania by Nicolls in honor of the Duke of York's domain of Albany in Scotland, gained a new name, Nova Caesaria, a Latin rendering of New Jersey, after the Isle of Jersey, the elder Carteret's birthplace, which he had defended for the king during the English Civil War. The Latin was dropped early on, although a later diagonal division into East and West Jersey resulted in the colony being known as "the Jerseys" for a while.

Young Carteret declared Nicolls's grants void, initiating a century-long squabble over property and politics. New Jersey would suffer through a maelstrom of internal dissension fueled by a complex process of land surrender and regrant, sale and resale of proprietorship rights, confusion of the demarcation between civil government and land ownership and the hated demands by the proprietors of the moment for the payment of medieval land occupation fees called "quitrents." Riots and political resistance to proprietary and then royal governors and their appointed officials became a fact of life in "the Jerseys" well into the eighteenth century. Despite the confusion and wrangling, however, the colony continued to grow and in 1683 Navesink Patent became Monmouth County.[14]

Although northern Monmouth County was fairly well settled, according to the standards of the time, by the middle of the eighteenth century, few people lived along the coast to the south, on the outer coastal plain, where soils in colonial days were regarded "very poor to poor." Although the immediate vicinity of today's Sea Girt fell into the slightly better "poor to fair" category, there was little to draw potential farmers arriving in Monmouth County to the shore. In 1765, coastal livelihoods included cattle raising, oyster gathering and whaling. Even these occupations were limited in the area of present-day Sea Girt. Although whales were taken along the coast from Sandy Hook south, whaling was only well established at Long Beach Island and Cape May, and most cattle were set out to graze on the barrier islands between bay and ocean to the south, while oyster gathering was best north and south of southern Monmouth County. Because of these factors "the Outer Coastal Plain remained essentially unoccupied in 1765."[15]

In the eighteenth century, few people traveled south of Shrewsbury and Middletown in Monmouth County. One such traveler was Church of England missionary Thomas Thompson. In 1746, after rectifying what he perceived to be theological disorder caused by the "bad influence" of "*Quakers* and *Anabaptists*" in northern Monmouth, Thompson ventured south along the coast. He found "some Church Families" clustered about Shark River, and a few more at Manasquan, where he baptized two African American men who were either free servants or slaves of Samuel Osbourn. Thompson reported that the country south of the Manasquan River was even worse—"all one Pine Forest and a Desart," where "Heathenism" abounded.[16]

Despite the quitrent riots and other disorders in New Jersey, the colony was not an epicenter of events leading up to the American Revolution. There was a general belief among Jerseyans, however, that Britain was interfering too much in colonial affairs, and these colonists exhibited some sympathy for the problems of Massachusetts, enough so that New Jersey had its own "tea party" in Greenwich in 1774. With the outbreak of hostilities in 1775, some New Jerseyans set up an unofficial government in opposition to royal Governor William Franklin (Benjamin's son), who remained loyal to the king. Franklin was arrested and confined by Patriot forces in 1776 but eventually was exchanged and became head of the Associated Loyalists, an organization whose coastal raiding made life miserable for Jersey Shore residents in the years to come. Although there were a number of significant battles in the state, enough to earn it the nickname "Cockpit of the Revolution," the day-in, day-out struggle was largely a guerilla campaign, often—as in places like Monmouth County, with its large number of Loyalists—a civil war with neighbor against neighbor.[17]

There is historical consensus that the Revolutionary War wrecked the New Jersey economy, but it provided economic opportunity for some. The few families living near Manasquan and Wreck Pond inlets in 1775 survived by cutting trees for lumber and to make charcoal and engaging in a bit of fishing and subsistence farming. Once the war came, however, they discovered they were sitting alongside one of the most critical of eighteenth-century military necessities—salt. Some believe sea salt was a component of gunpowder, but this is incorrect. The substance used in making gunpowder is potassium nitrate, sometimes confused with sodium nitrate, a salt mined in Chile that is also used in making explosives. The latter is, in turn, often confused with sodium chloride, or "table salt," distilled from the sea. Nonetheless, salt was an important strategic commodity since it was a requirement for preserving meat and fish. There had been a few local efforts to extract salt from bay water, most notably at Forked River in 1754, but no large-scale efforts in New Jersey prior to the Revolution. In the years before 1775, New Jersey's salt needs were satisfied with West Indies sea salt and rock salt from Massachusetts and Virginia.[18]

As early as 1688, entrepreneurs realized that the New Jersey coast provided "many convenient places" to make salt from seawater, but there was no significant motivation to do so until British blockading ships and invading armies disrupted trade routes. In December 1775 the Continental Congress advised colonial legislatures to encourage salt making, and in 1776 the *Pennsylvania Magazine* reprinted a portion of a 1748 work on salt making by Dr. William Brownrigg, which was widely circulated in pamphlet form. Subsequent legislation proposed bounties for salt production and established a Congressional Committee on the subject.[19]

In October 1776 the New Jersey legislature encouraged private individuals to erect salt making establishments along the coast, and a year later planned for a state saltworks. The latter idea was abandoned when it became clear that private efforts would suffice. A 1777 bill exempting workers in the salt and iron industries from militia duty ensured an ample workforce. Soon there were saltworks up and down the coast, "from the Shrewsbury River to Cape May." One of the biggest was the Union Saltworks, located on the Manasquan River in what is now Brielle. It and the other works were prime targets for Franklin's Loyalist raiders. In April 1778 it was reported that "about 135 of the enemy landed on Sunday last about 10 o'clock on the south side of Squan inlet, burnt all the salt-works, broke the kettles, etc, stripped the beds, etc. of some people there wished to serve them, then crossed the river and burnt all except Dirrick Longstreets; after this mischief they embarked." The same force attacked several saltworks at Shark River, with less success.[20]

The Union Saltworks was rebuilt and offered for sale a year later. Sales literature provides an insight into the equipment needed for salt production, listing property including a "pump house" with "pumps by which water from the bay [Manasquan River] is conveyed either immediately into the pans or into a covered cistern." Water was often left in the cistern to evaporate as a first stage in salt making prior to boiling, which took place in a "boiling house." The Union Saltworks had nine huge copper and iron pans for boiling salt water for the final extraction of salt. It was one of the largest employers in the area, and also sold imported salt from blockade runners.[21]

With the end of the Revolution and abundant and cheap imported salt, the Jersey Shore salt business collapsed, and by 1800 was only a memory. The beaches and inlets of lower Monmouth County slipped back into an economy of subsistence agriculture, fishing and other marginal rural pursuits, interrupted by a little excitement during the War of 1812, when British blockading ships hovered off the coast. As the nineteenth century progressed, however, people from Philadelphia and New York began to travel to the Jersey Shore for relaxation and sea bathing, even though available wagon and stagecoach routes were arduous. As years went by, boat tourism to Cape May and Long Branch increased, as did the growth of hotels and other businesses catering to the tourist trade.[22]

During the first half of the nineteenth century there were several local government changes in Monmouth County. In 1801, the southern portion of Shrewsbury Township became Howell Township, named for Governor Richard Howell, and in 1850 the southern portion of Monmouth County became Ocean County. In 1851, the land that would eventually be Sea Girt became part of Monmouth's Wall Township, carved out of Howell's coastal area and named for U.S. Senator Garett D. Wall.[23]

Even the out-of-the-way stretch of beach between the Shark and Manasquan Rivers began to see a few tourists, albeit not the first-class ones heading for Cape May and Long Branch. By the 1830s, "Squan Village," described as being "in the S.E. portion of Howell Township between Manasquan and Mattetecunk [*sic*] rivers," was "much frequented for sea-bathing," with "comfortable accommodations…found at the farmhouses, of which there are several where boarders are received." A decade later, Squan had "2 stores, a neat church and about 30 dwellings." Although primarily engaged in the coastal wood and charcoal trade, supplemented by some shipbuilding, the town was "much visited in the summer months for sea bathing," with "several boarding houses for the accommodation of visitors." The idea of the New Jersey Shore as a vacation spot had been born, and was beginning to grow.[24]

In the remaining years of the nineteenth century and the first decades of the twentieth, the beach north of Squan and then the town that came to be Sea Girt would slowly develop into one of the best-known resorts on the New Jersey coast. In the century following the Civil War, Sea Girt became home to luxurious hotels, the site of an annual rural ocean bathing expedition, a National Guard training camp and the summer residence of New Jersey's governors, who planned future political moves and hosted gala balls for the state's political and military elite. New Jersey's soldiers would go off to war from Sea Girt. Presidents visited Sea Girt, and candidates for president began their campaigns there at massive rallies organized by the most famous (some would say infamous) figure in twentieth-century New Jersey and American politics, Jersey City's mayor Frank Hague. Much of the vibrant story of that Sea Girt century is now forgotten, but deserves to be remembered. Sea Girt's name, as well as its place in New Jersey and United States history, all began with one man's choice to place his summer home on a largely barren stretch of coastal beach. That man—whose strut across the state and national stage in business, military and political venues made him one of the best-known personalities of his era—was Robert Field Stockton.

CHAPTER 2

The Commodore Buys a Farm

Robert Field Stockton was, at one time or another, a wealthy aristocrat, heroic naval officer, monopoly capitalist, self-interested political operative, social progressive and apologist for slavery. In the course of all these twists and turns, he became one of the most influential and controversial men in New Jersey and, indeed, America in the first half of the nineteenth century. A grandson of Richard Stockton, New Jersey signer of the Declaration of Independence, and son of United States Attorney, Congressman and Senator Richard Stockton, Robert was born in 1795 in Princeton. He attended the College of New Jersey (Princeton University) but discovered early on that academe paled before potential adventure and dropped out to join the navy as a midshipman at the age of sixteen. During the War of 1812, Stockton was cited for bravery and rose to the rank of lieutenant. In the postwar years he challenged British naval officers to duels when they showed insufficient respect for the American navy, fought Algerian and Caribbean pirates, captured slave ships and—as the representative of the American Colonization Society—penetrated deep West African rainforests and negotiated at pistol point with local chiefs to establish what would become Liberia, planned as a homeland for freed African American slaves.[25]

Richard Stockton died in 1828, leaving his son a "princely fortune." During the ensuing years, the younger Stockton took long leaves from naval service to become involved in other projects, both political and financial. Following the War of 1812, transportation issues came to the forefront in an expanding American economy, and Stockton had the foresight and organizational skills to capitalize on them while others dithered. In 1830, with money fronted by his wealthy South Carolina father-in-law John Potter, he purchased most of the stock of the Delaware and Raritan Canal, which he then merged with John Stevens's Camden and Amboy Railroad, forming the Joint Companies, a legislatively sanctioned monopoly that locked up the transportation of people and goods across New Jersey between Philadelphia and New York.[26]

The New Jersey Legislature granted the monopoly an exemption from all taxes, provided it paid a "transit duty of ten cents a passenger and fifteen cents a ton of merchandise" into the state treasury. Coincidentally, legislators received free passage on the Camden and Amboy Railroad. Once granted the monopoly, the Joint Companies engaged in a decades-long struggle to maintain it against both competitors and

Commodore Robert F. Stockton in 1840. *Courtesy Library of Congress.*

politicians who thought the state got a raw deal. In wringing every dollar possible out of absolute control of the passageway across New Jersey while it lasted, the Joint Companies interpreted the agreement to its own advantage, allegedly pulling every trick in the book to minimize transit duties to the state. Still, enough money was remitted to make the Joint Companies' fees the largest contributions to New Jersey's annual budget, allowing lawmakers to largely forego taxes for funds to run state government.

A serial political party switcher, Stockton was, over several decades, a member of the Federalist, National Republican, Democrat, Whig, Native American and Constitutional Unionist Parties, although most of the time he was a nominal Democrat. His lifelong political tap dance appears to have been motivated by personal and financial motives, not ideological ones, however. A Whig supporter of John Quincy Adams in 1824, he transferred his loyalty to the Democratic Party and Andrew Jackson in 1828, reportedly due to Adams's failure to appoint his father to a patronage position. Other changes of allegiance were apparently connected to the furtherance of the cause of the Joint Companies. Stockton and John Stevens were business and transportation entrepreneurs and innovators, but had no interest in a competitive marketplace. Much of Stockton's political activity was centered on bribing, lobbying and running employees for office to control the New Jersey Legislature in order to preserve the monopoly. The struggle went on for decades, until the state finally rescinded the agreement after Stockton's death.[27]

Leaving Stevens to fight the ongoing legislative battles of the Joint Companies, Stockton returned to active naval service as a captain in 1838, and subsequently met Swedish ship designer John Ericsson, whom he convinced to come to America and design a steam-powered ship using a screw propeller rather than a paddle wheel for propulsion. Stockton directly supervised much of the construction of the new vessel, the *Princeton*, which was launched in Philadelphia in 1843, and personally designed one of its cannons, referred to as the Peacemaker. On February 28, 1844, Captain Stockton took the *Princeton* for a pleasure cruise on the Potomac River with President John Tyler, his cabinet and two hundred guests aboard. The Peacemaker was successfully fired several times to entertain the guests, but then exploded and killed six people, including Secretary of State Abel Upshur, Secretary of the Navy Thomas Gilmer and the president's soon-to-be father-in-law. Tyler himself narrowly escaped death or injury. Twenty others were wounded, including Stockton, who sustained facial burns. A quickly held court of inquiry absolved the captain from all blame, although he was the sole designer of the defective gun. Stockton's political support for and friendship with President Tyler appears to have had an influence on the outcome. Despite the disaster, in the end Stockton's wooing of Ericsson paid off for the country, as the inventive Swede later designed the Civil War ironclad *Monitor*.[28]

The explosion that nearly wiped out the United States government may have slowed Captain Stockton down a step or two, but he quickly recovered. The 1846 outbreak of the Mexican War found him, an acting commodore, sailing north along the California coast on a mission to reinforce the American Pacific Squadron under Commodore John D. Sloat. On Stockton's arrival, the ailing Sloat, who had been nudging Mexican authorities in California to accept an American takeover through diplomacy rather

Stockton's Peacemaker explodes aboard the *Princeton*. *Courtesy U.S. Naval History Institute.*

than military action, turned over command to the New Jersey officer. In a series of actions that earned him a reputation with one historian as "vain, tactless, zenophobic [*sic*], and glory-thirsty," Stockton undid Sloat's careful work, inciting a rebellion among the Californios. Aided by Brevet Captain John C. Fremont and Colonel Stephen Watts Kearny of the army, however, Stockton put together a ragtag little force that effectively stifled the insurrection in a swift campaign displaying his usual personal courage and revealing a surprising mastery of land-based tactical skills for a naval officer. Following a disagreement over the reinstitution of California civil authority with Kearny, the commodore headed back east, and by 1848, segueing seamlessly into his political persona, was advocating the annexation of Mexico.[29]

In 1850, Stockton resigned from the navy and returned to New Jersey business and politics. By 1851, his wealth, family name, heroic military service and political connections forged through the Joint Companies' activities resulted in his election as a United States senator by the state legislature, which, in that era, decided who would serve in that office. Stockton resigned for murky reasons in 1853, and, although there can be no doubt he served the interests of the Joint Companies in Washington, he also gained a name as a social reformer by introducing legislation to end the practice of flogging in the navy. At least one newspaper characterized his speech on the subject as "absurd" political grandstanding by the "Quarter-deck Senator," however, claiming that flogging, although still on the books, was actually "among the things past" in the navy.[30]

Out of political office, the commodore (that is what most people called him, although he only held the rank temporarily during the Mexican War and was actually a captain when he resigned from the navy) remained president of the Joint Companies for the rest of his life and lived up to the large income the monopoly provided. In May 1853 he added a seaside farm in what was then Wall Township, New Jersey, to his other properties, which included Morven, the family estate in Princeton, and homes in Philadelphia, London and farther up the Jersey coast in Long Branch. According to one account, Stockton selected the Wall location "as a retreat from the busy life," and purchased the farm, which he named Seagirt, from Thomas Shearman (aka Sherman) for a summer residence. Dissatisfied with the old, yet spacious farmhouse already on the property, he soon built a large new oceanfront residence.[31]

An 1892 account of Stockton's seafront home, years after it had become the central section of the Beach House hotel, referred to it as "the only fine old mansion to be found on the entire coast from Sandy Hook to Cape May." Local lore had Stockton keeping "a strict watch on the ocean with his telescope…perhaps to look out for pirates, but more likely, to see that the men had properly holystoned the decks of his yacht, which he kept anchored near shore." Old residents told a reporter that in his heyday Stockton ran a busy estate at Seagirt, with "at least three houses filled with his family, his friends and his workmen." According to New Jersey historian John T. Cunningham, Stockton spent six weeks each summer at Seagirt, and when he arrived, "trailing behind his carriage came a parade of vehicles laden with children, grandchildren, friends, servants and friends' servants," along with "blooded horses which would exercise all summer on the ¾-mile track at the Stockton grounds." The commodore's entourage traveled east from Princeton "by way of the old Jamesburg road and the Freehold and Tuckerton post roads." Villagers, like medieval peasants of old, gathered along the roadside to see the imperious personage and his caravan pass by.[32]

There were few visitors to Seagirt, located in the "barren wastes above the Manasquan" and featuring "great stretches of scrub pines in every direction," in the 1850s, and it is safe to assume that most of them had some business or political dealings with Stockton. This was especially true, locals recalled, when "the Presidential bee buzzed in the Stockton bonnet" in the mid-1850s, when "the beach was hardly big enough to hold all the friends who gathered about the Commodore nor the tides strong enough to carry away the champagne corks." Set atop a bluff overlooking the ocean, the commodore's mansion, one hundred feet long and twenty-five feet in depth, with fifteen-foot-wide piazzas across both floors, had three large public rooms with fourteen-foot ceilings on the first floor, and bedrooms on the second floor. According to one account, one of Stockton's seaside retreat's piazzas "was rigged like a deck, with capstan, compass, cleats and davits from which life boats are suspended." It was also reported, somewhat fancifully, that "the mansion has a veritable ship's bottom, so that, were it to be carried away by the sea, it would ride the waves in gallant style." In fact, it was constructed as any other house of similar size would have been by builder John G. Stiles of Manasquan. The house was so close to the sea that Stockton's wife reportedly refused to spend a night there for fear it would be swept away by a sudden storm, and retreated to an inland home, the Cottage, at dusk of every day. That building, "partially destroyed" by a 1929 fire and then "entirely rebuilt with its famous chimney on the east end carefully preserved," today stands on Washington Boulevard as Rod's Olde Irish Tavern.[33]

Stockton's life at Seagirt was indeed good. He enjoyed racing his horses and, according to a letter attributed to his granddaughter, playing in a private bowling alley, but the siren song of public life kept calling the commodore. In 1856, political allies proposed his name as the Native American Party's candidate for president and also, even though he was a longtime Democrat, put out the word that he was an available presidential choice for the new Republican Party. Despite the champagne parties on the beach, however, Stockton soon realized there was no realistic hope he would become a viable presidential candidate, and withdrew his name. The Republicans eventually nominated his old California subordinate, John C. Fremont.[34]

Failure to secure the top prize in American politics did not entirely end Robert Stockton's political life, however. In January 1860, foreseeing the coming sectional storm, he expressed sympathy with the Southern viewpoint, insisting that New Jerseyans "speak substantial words of fraternity and encouragement" to Southerners and insist that the Fugitive Slave Law be strictly enforced. By early 1861, with secession of the Deep South a reality, Stockton asked the state to use its influence to "supplicate the North to yield" to Southern demands in order to save the union, and served as a New Jersey delegate to a multistate Peace Conference held in Washington in February in an attempt at mediation between the federal government and the seceding states. Other conference participants were his friend, former President (and future Confederate Congressman) John Tyler, and former navy subordinate and ex-New Jersey Governor, Congressman and vocal Southern sympathizer Rodman Price. The group, representing twenty-one states, failed to achieve a satisfactory resolution, making the Civil War inevitable.[35]

Despite his initial Southern sympathies, during the 1863 Gettysburg campaign Stockton was appointed to command the New Jersey Militia by his son Robert, the state's adjutant general. Had General Robert E. Lee reached the Delaware River, there is no doubt he would have found the commodore glowering at him from the Jersey side, leading, despite his age, from the front. Robert F. Stockton lived to see the conflict end in Northern victory, but after the war bade farewell to Seagirt. On July 9, 1866, he swapped 225 acres of the tract "on the north side of Sea Girt Avenue extending north to Wreck Pond bounded on the east by the ocean" with Paul and Stephen Thurlow of Wilkes Barre, Pennsylvania, in exchange for "4,000 shares of the Capital Stock of the Plymouth Coal Company, Wyoming Valley, Luzerne County, Pa." Stockton returned to Morven, where he died that October 7 of "cholera morbus," a nineteenth-century term for what today is called acute gastroenteritis. The commodore aroused strong emotions during his lifetime and those who knew him either loved or hated him. In summing up his life a *New York Times* obituary put it this way: "He could not be a common man, put him where you would; and he was, above all, intensely a Jerseyman."[36]

Although the Thurlows did lease some of their new land for farming, agriculture was not their ultimate intent. They predicated a return on their investment from post–Civil War prosperity and the expansion of the railroad network, creating new possibilities for summer vacation resort communities. Seagirt farm, the Thurlow brothers believed, would become the new vacationland of "Sea Girt." In 1867 the Freehold and Jamesburg Railroad's Farmingdale and Squan Village branch completed its line to Squan, a short

Commodore Stockton in 1861.
Courtesy National Archives and Records Administration.

carriage ride away. The completion provided the final link in a series of railroads that connected with the Camden and Amboy at Jamesburg, thus providing a rail route from Philadelphia to the shore. A subsequent *New York Times* article touted the new community of Sea Girt's "beautiful position and attractive surroundings." The story credited Sea Girt with "a beach unsurpassed for bathing purposes and drives as varied and beautiful as any lover of nature could desire," ensuring its "future popularity as a watering place." According to the *Times*, a work crew was "employed in opening the avenues and constructing the principal boulevard," with "arrangements in progress for building cottages of every description."[37]

In 1868, Robert Stockton's heirs were sued for failure to pay a $43,780 debt and the Thurlows added eleven more adjacent tracts of the late commodore's land, totaling over three hundred acres, to their original Seagirt farm property by purchasing it at a Monmouth County sheriff's sale. Despite the new railroad and the publicity, however, development was slow. In a labyrinthine series of land deals of a type that persisted for the rest of the century, Paul Thurlow transferred his interest in the property to Stephen in 1871, and in 1875 Stephen sold the whole five hundred acres to the Sea Girt Land Improvement Company, a corporation that included both brothers as officers. No doubt hoping to accelerate the progress of the resort project, the company hired an engineer, Charles F. Ingham, to lay out building lots and streets and signed on New Jersey Attorney General and former Governor Joel Parker as an officer for a little political insurance. Parker's contribution is unrecorded, but Ingham's fan-like street pattern radiated out from a semicircular woodlot called Crescent Park, which fronted on the ocean. The design proved impractical and the street plat was changed to a conventional gridiron pattern in 1877 by another engineer, Frederick J. Anspach. Anspach did not disturb Crescent Park, however, and it remains, to this day, the only relic of the original town layout still extant.[38]

Once a town plan was established, the new development company produced a sales brochure pitched at Pennsylvanians declaring that "Lots & Villa Sites" were available at Sea Girt, "10 miles south of Long Branch," which was "nearer Philadelphia than Cape May or Long Branch." Potential buyers were lured by the prospectus's claims of "fertile soil" and a beachfront "timbered with a heavy growth of oak, pine, cedar, etc." Despite the publicity, only eight lots were sold in 1875–76, all of them in front of Crescent Park, and all but one to Charles S. Taylor of Burlington, New Jersey, to Pennsylvanians. The hotel business proved more lucrative. During 1878–80, Paul Thurlow and his wife Mary opened the Tremont House in conjunction with fellow Philadelphian Thomas Gregg, and Thomas Devlin established the Parker House, both located in the northern part of town. Devlin's hostelry bucked the trend for out of area ownership, as he was from Manasquan and was locally well known as "a chef of considerable renown." All of Sea Girt's hotels courted the carriage trade. New Yorker Colonel Lucius U. Maltby promoted his high-end Beach House, with the old Stockton shoreline mansion as its central section, as "lighted with gas throughout and supplied with baths on every floor and all modern conveniences."[39]

There is no doubt that the investors of the Sea Girt Land Improvement Company wanted to make their new town a classy enterprise. An early deed for property sold to Pennsylvanian Hibbard Yarnall specifies that "no blacksmith shop, livery stable, glue, soap, candle, gas or starch manufacturing, carpenter shop, slaughter house or other building for offensive occupations shall be erected or used upon the above described lot of ground," and the same restrictions appear in all subsequent deeds. They soon thought better of Ingham's Crescent Park, however, proposing that streets be driven through it to free up more lots for sale. This effort was strenuously opposed by people who had bought beachfront property with the park providing a miniprimeval pocket of privacy for their backyards. Yarnall and Philadelphian Elliston P. Morris, who owned property in front of the park, filed lawsuits against the company on several occasions, and in 1884 gained a permanent injunction against changing the park's configuration.[40]

No matter the street scheme of the planned town of Sea Girt, or its promotion by successive owners, lot sales remained desultory. In 1881, Hunterdon County's *Hopewell Herald* described Sea Girt as "a new village—small and straggling." Eight years later, tour book author Gustave Kobbe noted that the town had "but few permanent residents, they being farmers or fishermen along the shore of Wrack [*sic*] Pond, known also as Sea Girt inlet." He also remarked that "very few cottages" had been built and that hotels

The Beach House hotel. *Courtesy Randy Gabrielan.*

The Tremont Hotel. *Courtesy Randy Gabrielan.*

The Parker House. *Courtesy of the author.*

housed most of Sea Girt's summer visitors. Another account described Sea Girt in 1885 as consisting "principally of a few farm houses and the Beach House." Founded by Pennsylvanians and initially more accessible from Philadelphia than New York City by rail, most of the Beach House's guests were, unsurprisingly, well-to-do residents of that Pennsylvania metropolis, and Kobbe noted that "if you shake the genealogical tree of a Sea Girt summer visitor, a Binney or a Biddle is sure to drop off." Access to Sea Girt from New York greatly improved in the spring of 1876, when the New York and Long Branch Railroad, leased by and directly connected to the New Jersey Central Railroad at Elizabeth, extended its tracks south, connecting with the Freehold and Jamesburg, which was leased to the Pennsylvania Railroad, just outside of town. Eventually two stations would be built: one, which still stands as the Sea Girt Library, for the New York and Long Branch, where travelers from the North would arrive, and another, long gone, at the junction of the two roads where vacationers from Philadelphia and points west would debark. In the 1880s Colonel Maltby, never missing a chance to promote his establishment, proposed that if the New York and Long Branch could run a train from Jersey City to Sea Girt in ninety minutes, he would guarantee that 150 Wall Street brokers would ride it to and from the Beach House. The New York trip actually took around two hours, and travelers from Philadelphia arrived in a few minutes less time.[41]

Aside from hotel luxury and the ocean itself, a significant tourist attraction for Binneys, Biddles, perhaps even the Morrises and other summer sojourners in late nineteenth-century Sea Girt was watching the activities at Salt Water Day, or Beach Day. Held on the second Saturday in August, Salt Water Day was an event drawing farmers from as far as thirty miles inland to the shore to picnic on the beach and splash in the ocean near Wreck Pond. No one quite knew the holiday's origins, but after the Civil War, when the annual surf safari first came to the attention of journalists, it was attributed to an Indian custom of traveling across the state to the beach for a summer shellfish feast. Local Native Americans did harvest fish and shellfish along the coast, primarily at Raritan Bay, but also at Manasquan inlet and perhaps Wreck Pond, before the coming of Europeans, but the story of long-distance pilgrimages to do so has no foundation in fact. Atlantic Highlands historian Paul D. Boyd, who has made a study of the legend, convincingly argues that it is "bunk." Any relationship between the customs of nineteenth-century farmers and Lenape is tenuous at best.

In 1882 a "lately deceased" Spring Lake resident was quoted as saying, with no mention of Indian antecedents, that he had "gone to Wreck Pond on 'big day' when a small boy, over fifty years ago." A 1922 Monmouth County history noted, with no references to Native Americans, that "for many years prior to 1853 the shores of what is now Sea Girt was the place where the farmers and other inhabitants of this section met to celebrate their annual harvest home festivals." A 1939 account referred to a still-celebrated annual Salt Water Day at Keyport as "having its origin more than a hundred years ago, when farmers made a yearly holiday visit to the seashore." This source also seems to discount a lineal Indian or colonial precedent, but does assert that "the custom is believed to have been inspired by Indian clambakes on the beach." As noted previously, cultural contact between early settlers and native residents of the area was a one-way street, limited to land purchases and employment as paid hunters and fishermen for a few years. An 1887 *Harper's Weekly* article reported that "along the Jersey shore, farmers living within twenty or thirty miles felt a keen oyster hunger about the first of every August," apparently disregarding the rule of thumb that oysters be eaten in the "r" months. Legislation of 1719 forbidding the harvesting of oysters between May 10 and September 1 makes the theory of colonial precedence even more unlikely. Substantive evidence of any direct connection between Native American practices, culinary and otherwise, and those of future generations of Monmouth County farmers is lacking, and the custom of Salt Water Day appears to have its origins in the nineteenth century. It is likely, however, that at least some participants believed they were, in some fashion, reenacting an ancient rite, a rationale that passed into local folklore, although we will probably never know the true origins of Salt Water Day.[42]

Vague as they are, it seems that the beginnings of Salt Water Day may well have been farther north, as the Keyport reference indicates. Another account refers to a "bathing day," when Middlesex County rural folk traveled as many as twenty miles to Raritan Bay at South Amboy following the August full moon. A *Frank Leslie's Illustrated Newspaper* of August 29, 1868, featured an illustration of fully clothed rural folk cavorting in the water at South Amboy as part of what the periodical referred to as a "Harvest Home Festival." The farmers were apparently as rowdy as any college frat boys on spring break, and an 1856 story reporting more than two thousand "persons of all ages, sexes and colors" returning from Raritan Bay noted euphemistically that the behavior of the participants was "highly unconventional."[43]

Whatever the custom's origins and alternate locations, in the late nineteenth century Wreck Pond inlet became the site of the biggest Salt Water Day on the New Jersey coast, and an 1882 account cited "at least 6,000 persons" celebrating there. On August 14, 1886, over five hundred wagons were counted on the Sea Girt sand, with many other people arriving for the festivities by train. As the century waned, Salt Water Day began to attract the attention of city journalists writing to amuse an upscale urban audience. An 1885 *New York Times* correspondent advised city sophisticates that "in bright calico and gingham the farmers' wives and daughters were dressed, while some of the men wore the brass buttoned blue coats they don only on festal days and Presidential election day, when they go to the polls to vote for Andrew Jackson." In 1893, the same newspaper described ocean-bathing farmers at Sea Girt using "their overalls for suits," while their "women folk put on calico wrappers." That year two "deacons of a Baptist church in the Ocean County Pines," who imbibed too freely in available "drinkables," got into a fistfight on the beach over the free coinage of silver issue and "country lads and maidens" danced to the music of one Jinks Beatty, who "wuz the best all-round fiddler this side o' Phildelfy." One participant recalled that a man named Charlie Anderson brought a box of rattlesnakes he had caught in the Pine Barrens to the Sea Girt beach, and charged people ten cents to take a look at them.[44]

In 1895, with Salt Water Day celebrated at both South Amboy and Sea Girt, the roisterous rubes at Wreck Pond were accused of making so much noise after arrival on Friday night "that many of the residents were disturbed and could not sleep." By that time, Salt Water Day had evolved into a full-scale carnival:

> *After taking dips in the ocean, the farmers and their families rested on the sand. Fakirs from New-York and elsewhere reaped a harvest from the unsuspecting farmers while they were on the shore. The man selling pies also got a good share of the money. Many young men and women strolled along the beach with pies in one hand and frankfurters in the other. At noon, everybody ate luncheon. The merry-go-round, rifle range and a doll target were well patronized.*[45]

A 1901 *Trenton Times* correspondent noted that there was "no style nor nonsense about the horny handed grangers and their buxom wives and sweethearts from the pines" who assembled on the Wreck Pond beach. He condescendingly added that "4,000 to 5,000 grangers" had shown up at Sea Girt "to take their annual bath."[46]

The urban vacationers who began to establish summer bungalow communities in the New Jersey Shore resorts in the early years of the twentieth century gradually grew more annoyed than amused by the rural antics of the "horny handed grangers" on Salt Water Day. In 1905, a number of Sea Girt summer residents requested that the festival be moved to nearby Manasquan. By 1956, when eminent New Jersey folklorist Henry Charlton Beck investigated the custom, he noted that there had not been a legitimate Salt Water Day, occasionally called Big Sea Day, in "more than twenty years." Beck interviewed McClelland Estlow, an old man who participated in the holiday in his prime and referred to it as Farmer's Wash Day or Beach Day. Estlow recalled that the main

Salt Water Day, circa 1900. *Courtesy Sea Girt Lighthouse.*

celebration "used to be held about where Spring Lake is," but that it had come to an end because "different kind of people came in, people from the cities that wanted to build shacks, anything at all, so they could splash around and have a Big Sea Day every day."[47]

Salt Water Day was never mentioned in any official Sea Girt publicity as an attraction, and there is evidence that the town's hotels wished the farmers would go away. A newspaper report as early as 1885 advised that most hostelries posted "No 'sea folks' admitted" signs over their doors come mid-August. Save for some commercialized adaptations as Big Sea Day by neighboring resorts in the post–World War II era, the farmers' holiday at Sea Girt gradually faded into history and folklore. More and more people wanted Estlow's "Big Sea Day every day," and that desire, along with New Jersey's need for a National Guard rifle range, would finally bring Sea Girt the resort status the Land Improvement Company had dreamed of a generation before—and much more.[48]

CHAPTER 3
The National Guard Comes to Town

The New Jersey National Guard was formed out of New Jersey Militia and New Jersey Rifle Corps units in 1869 in an effort to create a better organized, more efficient state military force. Many of the reorganized Guard's officers had military experience in the Civil War, and, in common with a lot of other veterans of that conflict, were appalled by the lack of marksmanship ability of the men they commanded. As a partial remedy, they initiated a program in 1869 intended to reward good shots by offering marksmanship medals, which were awarded following the Guard's first shooting competition held in Newark that year.[49]

During the 1870s and 1880s, Guardsmen practiced at rented ranges, including the Stockton Range outside of Camden and the Brinton Range near Elizabeth. Since both ranges were privately owned by civilian shooting clubs, they were not always available. By the mid-1880s, the lack of a permanent shooting venue, as well as an area to assemble units to practice drill and maneuvers, was a matter of concern to Adjutant General William S. Stryker, a Civil War veteran who believed the National Guard should be well drilled and able to shoot well in case of a national emergency. In his annual report for 1882, Stryker commented that "no better plan can now be devised than for the State to select some permanent summer camping ground for her troops," and urged legislative action on the subject. In 1883, General Bird W. Spencer, New Jersey's inspector general of rifle practice, seconded Stryker, pointing out that renting the Brinton range cost the state $3,000 a season.[50]

Centrally located southern coastal Monmouth County, accessible by rail from most of the state yet still relatively undeveloped, seemed a potential campsite area that would fulfill Stryker and Spencer's requirements. And so the New Jersey National Guard first came "down the shore" in August 1884, when the state's Second Brigade held a summer encampment at Manasquan. The site was named Camp Abbett in honor of then-Governor Leon Abbett, setting a precedent for naming future camps after sitting governors. It was occupied from August 18 through 23 under the command of Irish-born Brevet Major General William J. Sewell. Sewell, a Pennsylvania Railroad executive, Republican Party boss of Camden and former state senator who was also a United States senator at the time, was a Civil War veteran who had served as colonel of the Fifth and Thirty-eighth New Jersey Infantry Regiments and had been wounded at Gettysburg.

In 1896, Sewell was awarded the Medal of Honor for his actions at Chancellorsville in May of 1863. In 1884, his brigade included the Third, Sixth and Seventh New Jersey National Guard Infantry Regiments and Gatling gun Company B.[51]

Sewell's camp was located "on Main Street, on the lands of Capt. William H. Bailey and Mr. Osborne Curtis, below the central railroad station." Adjoining property was rented for use as a rifle range, providing Guardsmen with an opportunity to fire their .45-70 caliber Model 1873 Springfield rifles at distances of two hundred, three hundred and five hundred yards. Manasquan seemed an ideal summer training venue for the state's military. The Freehold *Monmouth Democrat* editorialized that "this will be one of the largest and finest encampments ever held in the State of New Jersey and will attract visitors from all parts of the State and adjacent cities. The means of access by the public lines of travel being easy and cheap."[52]

Although the 1884 campground was leased, it was apparent that a permanent establishment was desirable, and that the Monmouth County coast was the best location. General Sewell reported that "the state should own its own ground, put up some permanent buildings for cook-houses, quartermasters' stores, stables etc. etc." A permanent campground, Sewell believed, would "keep our National Guard up to that state of efficiency that we can point to it with pride, as we have done in the past, as an organization competent to perform its duty, and ready at all times to take the field."[53]

In accordance with Sewell's conclusions, over the winter of 1884–85 the state settled on a section of Sea Girt, slightly north of the 1884 campsite, for use beginning in the summer of 1885. The New Jersey Assembly subsequently authorized R.S. Jenkins of Camden and W.T. Hoffman of Jersey City to act as agents in acquiring 120 acres of ground in Sea Girt, which the legislators proposed to condemn for government use at a compensation rate of $425 an acre. The land, part of the parcel the Thurlows had acquired at the 1868 sheriff's sale, was intended to serve a dual use: as a summer camp for the National Guard and as an encampment site for the New Jersey posts of the Grand Army of the Republic, the Civil War Union Veterans' Organization. Governor Abbett believed "the amount saved by the State in using the camp for a rifle range will in ten years be sufficient to pay for the land, improve the same and erect necessary buildings." Despite the governor's enthusiasm, the purchase bill faced rougher sledding in the state senate, where opposition to the condemnation proceedings postponed acquisition of the property.[54]

The state leased the land for the 1885 encampment, the first conducted at Sea Girt, from the Sea Girt Land Improvement Company for an annual rental of $3,000 until purchase-enabling legislation could be passed. Some Sea Girt landowners opposed the sale, and reproduced in pamphlet form an Asbury Park *Shore Press* story criticizing the "enormous" price of $600 an acre the company now asked for the property, while railing against the fiscal irresponsibility of using taxpayer money for "furnishing the militia of the state a grand annual spree." Conceding that some Guardsmen attending camp "conducted themselves like gentlemen," the article noted that "the great majority of the men who were at Sea Girt last summer came for nothing else but to have a good time, and they had it." Lax discipline, the story claimed, resulted in "stage loads of 'soldiers' crazy drunk, and singing and yelling at the full strength of their lungs, returning from some of the low saloons and disorderly houses at Manasquan, Neptune City or the suburbs of Asbury Park." A nostalgic account of the 1885 encampment printed three decades later did indeed recall that the troops interpreted the sounding of "Taps" as "a signal to begin merrymaking." According to the *Press*, the local people would "prefer that the State camp be located at the other end of the state." Opposition to the National Guard camp appears to have been led by Elliston Morris and a few other Sea Girt property owners from Philadelphia who had little patience for "the use of the ground for military purposes, with its unnecessary accompaniments of soldiers, visitors and the attendant annoyance." Morris filed a lawsuit claiming, in essence, that sale of the camp property to the state would impinge on his rights for future access and sewage connections, although the fact that he was a prominent Quaker may well have been a contributing factor in his opposition to a military base in Sea Girt. The suit was dismissed.[55]

Morris and friends to the contrary, the state had its way. Abbett's successor, Governor Robert S. Green, pushed ahead on the sale. One source states that the purchase was finally concluded in 1887 during Green's administration, for a sum of $51,000, by appointed commissioners James Smith Jr. of Newark and William L. Dayton of Trenton. Both men were prominent Democrats, and Smith would later become a New Jersey United States senator. Another account maintains the land was not finally acquired until 1891, during Governor Abbett's second term, by Judge John G. Trusdell of Essex County and Edward Bettle of Camden. An 1887 newspaper editorial suggests the earlier date is correct and lists the price paid to the Sea Girt Land Improvement Company as "about fifty-four thousand dollars."[56]

According to Adjutant General Stryker, the Sea Girt site was personally selected by Governor Abbett. Leon Abbett was one of New Jersey's first hands-on chief executives, and perhaps the greatest of its nineteenth-century governors, a Jersey City Democrat who helped integrate immigrants into the political system, advocated fair taxation of railroads and promoted early civil rights legislation. After consultation with the "principal officers of the National Guard interested in the subject," Stryker agreed with the governor, and wrote that he believed "it would be difficult…to find another site as suitable, combining the natural advantages for a Brigade or even Division camp, with ample parade ground, singularly adequate facilities for rifle range purposes and the advantages of safe surf bathing under proper restrictions." The state subsequently added a small parcel of land in 1907, but there is no formal record of the original sale extant today.[57]

According to Monmouth County folklore, the current National Guard Training Center was leased or sold by the Stockton family to the State of New Jersey with a proviso that the land would revert to the family should it cease to be used for military purposes. There is no basis for this assertion. As noted in the previous chapter, the property was owned by the Sea Girt Land Improvement Company, a group of Philadelphia investors, and had not belonged to anyone in the Stockton family for almost two decades when it was acquired by the state. The facts are simple. Robert Stockton transferred half of his farm to the Thurlow brothers in 1866 and his heirs were forced to sell the remainder of the land at a sheriff's sale to satisfy a large debt two years later. The Thurlows bought that acreage as well and then sold the whole parcel to the Sea Girt Land Improvement Company, in which they were officers, in 1875. An examination of all the property transfers to that date fails to reveal any sort of reversion clause.[58]

Despite the lack of surviving transaction records concerning the purchase of the property by the state, there is no doubt that the National Guard was firmly established at Sea Girt from 1885 on, with encampments of varying length held every year. In 1889, travel writer Gustav Kobbe noted that "the State camp, where the N.G.S.N.J. [National Guard State of New Jersey] holds its annual field exercises during one week in August, is a beautiful tract of land whose entrance is near the [railroad] station. The glamour and bustle of military life and the ball given at the Beach House to the Governor and his staff make the encampment a welcome episode of the summer season."[59]

The New Jersey National Guard at Sea Girt in 1888. *Courtesy NGMMNJ.*

In 1885, the National Guard began its Sea Girt encampment on August 15. Governor Abbett himself spent time under canvas with the troops, albeit in a large tent with a wooden floor. Good attendance was guaranteed by the fact that this was the first encampment that soldiers were paid to attend. According to Stryker, "The men received daily instruction in skirmish drill and in the rifle practice incident thereto." In addition, the adjutant general noted that "the gun [boat howitzer] squads recently formed and attached to some of the regiments have already attained an excellent degree of discipline. The gun practice at a floating target at sea gave the men a new and interesting experience in gunnery." The gunners fired at a canvas target floating on a raft eight hundred yards off the beach. Despite the grumbling of Mr. Morris about after-hours activities, the camp layout, discipline and drill of the Guardsmen displayed when on duty impressed a number of visitors from New York, including members of that state's prestigious Seventh Regiment Veteran Association. A grand review of Sewell's Brigade was followed by the first, precedent-setting Sea Girt military ball, given by Governor Abbett.[60]

Abbett's ball, held at the Beach House on August 21, was the most impressive affair of the New Jersey Shore 1885 summer season. It was remembered as "a brilliant event" to which "invitations numbering nearly 2,000 had been issued, distinguished men and women from various parts of the country lending their presence to the festivities." Less distinguished visitors to the camp had to make do with the carnival-like festivities "along

Governor Leon Abbett and military staff at Sea Girt, circa 1890. *Courtesy NGMMNJ.*

the main avenue, then but a lane, ungraded and with a heavy growth of pine scrubs," where "fakirs and others had erected stands, giving more the appearance of a country fair than a military encampment." The public was also entertained by the troops, who held dress parades every evening, accompanied by a bevy of private bands hired by the different regiments, including "famous" organizations like "Voss's band of Newark, Markwith's band of Orange and [the] Scranton [Pennsylvania] Brass Band."[61]

As the 1880s progressed, the National Guard, reflecting trends in the post–Civil War regular army, became more interested in long-range shooting. The New Jersey Guard's inspector general of marksmanship, General Spencer, a noted rifleman in his own right, recommended that the Sea Girt range be leveled and uniformly covered with sod, with a timber framework backstop behind the targets. He also suggested installing a fence to prevent "people from straying on the range" during shooting sessions. Spencer initiated the Governor's Match at Sea Girt in 1888, in which each competitor fired five shots each at two hundred and five hundred yards. Competition was keen, and the first winner was Major R. Heber Brientnall. In succeeding years, Spencer added more special events with valuable prizes, including Winchester and Remington rifles. The Guard also sent representatives to interstate rifle matches held at other locations, including those of the National Rifle Association held at Creedmoor, Long Island. Governor Abbett, a rifleman himself, posted a creditable score at Manasquan in 1884, and the New Jersey State Rifle Association was formed in Abbett's Trenton office in 1891, with the governor as its first president. The association subsequently established its headquarters at Sea Girt.[62]

Sea Girt rifle range, early twentieth century. *Courtesy Randy Gabrielan.*

New Jersey Rifle Association Headquarters, circa 1914. *Courtesy Randy Gabrielan.*

While Leon Abbett was the most interesting and significant political personality to frequent nineteenth-century Sea Girt, the town and camp saw their share of colorful and somewhat eccentric visitors as well. One of the most notable of these characters was Civil War veteran, Medal of Honor winner and National Guard officer James Madison Drake. During the Civil War, Drake, a lieutenant in the Ninth New Jersey Infantry, was captured at the battle of Drewry's Bluff, Virginia, on May 16, 1864, while fighting a holding action to prevent the Union right flank from being overrun. He escaped from a Confederate prison train near Charleston, South Carolina, on October 5, 1864, and, secretly aided by slaves, succeeded in making a several-hundred-mile overland trek to the safety of Union lines in Knoxville, Tennessee.[63]

After the war, Drake moved to Elizabeth, founded the *Daily Monitor* newspaper and joined the New Jersey National Guard, serving as colonel of the Third Regiment for five years. On leaving active National Guard service he was made a brevet (honorary) brigadier general by "special Act of the New Jersey Legislature" and ever afterward styled himself "General Drake." In 1867, Drake organized a drill team and fraternal organization called the Veteran Zouaves. The group—with three Medal of Honor winners, including Drake, in its ranks—wore uniforms patterned on those of the French North African soldiers who had inspired such admiration for their fine conduct in the Crimean War of 1854 to 1856 and the French campaign in Italy against the Austrians in 1859 that their drill and dress were widely imitated during the American Civil War. By 1908, Drake claimed his men had "made more pleasure excursions and visited more cities than any other military command in the country."[64]

J. Madison Drake. *Courtesy of the author.*

Such an organization needed a headquarters, so in the late 1870s Drake rejoined the New Jersey National Guard as a captain, bringing his Zouaves along with him as members of Gatling Gun Company A, for which the state provided an armory. When the captain and his men brought their Gatling guns to Sea Girt, they provided a colorful highlight to parades and acquitted themselves reasonably well on the range. The company, however, routinely defied the administrative rules of the National Guard. In 1889, an inspecting officer visiting the unit's Elizabeth armory reported that the company had no "company book neither any document of any sort," and observed that Drake's men "never adopted the state uniform."[65]

By the summer of 1892, although his company was still receiving inspection ratings of "fair" to "good," Drake had sufficiently irked the powers that be in the New Jersey National Guard, especially the Guard's division commander, General Joseph W.

Plume, that there was a concentrated effort to remove both him and his Zouaves from the state rolls. A general reorganization of the National Guard and disbandment of several infantry companies gave Plume his chance to get rid of Drake, whose company was added to the list of those to be disbanded. Drake and his Veteran Zouaves kept marching on as a veteran organization, however, and appeared at a Grand Army of the Republic encampment at Sea Girt in 1908.[66]

As the century wound down and the Civil War veterans in New Jersey National Guard ranks began to fade away, the Guard set its sights on fielding bigger guns than Drake's Gatlings. In 1884, Adjutant General Stryker suggested to Governor Abbett that the Guard, basically an infantry force with some small howitzers and Gatling guns, should procure heavy artillery from the federal government for training in sea coast defense. Stryker repeated the suggestion the following year, citing an article in the Newark *Press* that remarked that "it would be very easy for the Federal Government to erect some sort of a fortification at Sea Girt and man it with several patterns of heavy ordnance for the use of the National Guard."[67]

The guns were long in arriving, short in service and largely forgotten by the middle years of the twentieth century. On June 24, 2006, however, Mr. Robert H. Bossett of Brielle, New Jersey, visited the National Guard Militia Museum of New Jersey (NGMMNJ) at Sea Girt and donated copies of photographs he had taken on the beach at the Sea Girt National Guard Training Center following "the [September 21] 1938 hurricane." The pictures revealed two large coast artillery pieces, mounted on barbette carriages, and two smaller mortars. According to Bossett, the guns were buried in sand prior to the storm, when high winds uncovered them. He noted that he sold one of the pictures to the *Newark Sunday News* magazine for a dollar. Bossett stated that he was unaware of what had happened to the artillery pieces in the following years.[68]

Veteran Zouaves, Sea Girt, 1908. Drake is at left. *Courtesy John Kuhl.*

Rodman guns on beach, 1938. *Courtesy Bossett/NGMMNJ.*

An oral history interview of Korean War veteran Thomas Branch conducted in 2002 at the NGMMNJ confirmed Bossett's story. Branch's grandparents moved to Sea Girt in 1933. He was at their home in the autumn of 1938 and recalled that on the morning after the storm "we woke up to find Civil War cannons exposed on the beach." Branch recalled that this was a surprise, as he was not aware of their existence since they had been covered with sand until that time.[69]

The cannons in the pictures were on the beach in front of a sea wall at the rear of the rifle range, pointed seaward. The full extent of the carriages and gun emplacements was not revealed in the images, as the cannons remained covered with sand. An examination of the photographs revealed that the heavy artillery pieces were large-caliber muzzleloading Rodman guns intended for coastal defense, designed by Lieutenant Thomas J. Rodman, who at the time was commander of the Allegheny Arsenal.[70]

A witness to the unfortunate February 1844 explosion of Robert Stockton's Peacemaker aboard the USS *Princeton*, Rodman decided to find a better way to cast large-bore cannon that could sustain heavy powder charges. He patented his process in 1847 but continued to experiment, in conjunction with the Fort Pitt Foundry in Pittsburgh, to improve his gun's design. At the outbreak of the Civil War, Rodman received an order to produce a fifteen-inch-bore cannon based on his work. By 1864, Rodman guns in fifteen-, ten- and eight-inch bores began to replace older ordnance mounted in United States seacoast forts.[71]

Although the New Jersey National Guard inspector general reported to Adjutant General Stryker in 1887 that a newly formed Sea Coast Artillery Company in Atlantic City had passed inspection, no mention of heavy ordnance was made in the report. Two years later, however, General Stryker advised then-Governor Green that "we will soon be ready to apply to the War Department for the issue of ordnance and the erection of a battery on the shore land of the State Camp Ground." By that time the company in Atlantic City had been disbanded and the state's artillery force consisted of light howitzer gun crews, or "detachments," attached to National Guard infantry regiments. Stryker wanted these light artillerymen to be instructed to man heavy guns should the need arise, although there is no evidence this training occurred.[72]

The battery the state wanted did not arrive at Sea Girt until early 1896. Inspector General Joseph W. Congdon reported in October of that year that

> *on the twenty-fifth of May last, I repaired to Sea Girt with Brigadier-General* [Richard A.] *Donnelley, Quartermaster General, and after an inspection of the Sea-Coast battery erected at that place by Captain W.D. Ayres, of the United States Army, upon the order of the United States War Department, I took possession of it on behalf of the State of New Jersey…The Battery consists of one ten-inch Dahlgren* [sic] *gun, and two 12-inch mortars, properly mounted and protected by earthworks…It adds an interesting and instructive feature to grounds which are everywhere recognized as the finest property anywhere available and adaptable for camp and rifle practice.*[73]

Robert Bossett's photos reveal—in addition to the fact that Ayres actually installed a Rodman, not a Dahlgren gun—that there are two guns emplaced, not one, along with two mortars. Most likely the second gun was installed afterward. The Rodman 10-inch gun's barrel weighed approximately fifteen thousand pounds and had a barrel length of 136.66 inches. Rodmans were originally smoothbore artillery pieces firing a round ball projectile, but 210 of the 10-inch guns were sleeved with 8-inch bore diameter inserts cut with rifling to fire elongated projectiles between 1876 and 1887. Rifling added to the guns' range and accuracy. While it is possible that the Sea Girt guns were among this group, it is difficult to determine from the photographs if this was so.[74]

In 1897, Brigadier General Spencer requested that "the gun detachments of the various regiments be instructed in the manning and operation of the sea coast battery now built at Sea Girt…under the supervision of a United States Army artillery officer." In 1900, General Congdon suggested that "jetties, for the protection of the seashore, the seacoast batteries and the rifle pits from the inroads of the ocean should be built." New Jersey's seacoast battery, however, was already obsolete. An 1886 federal study called for a new coastal defense system featuring powerful breech-loading artillery pieces sited in dispersed and heavily reinforced concrete and armored gun positions. Installation of these weapons began during the 1890s and lasted into the early twentieth century.[75]

Although capable of firing a 125-pound projectile to a range of three miles, the Rodman guns mounted on the Sea Girt shore were never intended to defend against an enemy fleet, as were those sited in the forts around New York Harbor. Rather, they were instituted as training tools for National Guardsmen who might, in time of war, be called up to garrison federal coastal forts. Although outmoded as soon as they were built, they quickly became, as General Congdon noted, "an interesting and instructive feature" for visitors to the National Guard Training Center. They remained so, as evidenced by a 1916 photo of children posing in the gun position, until they were covered with sand and, sometime between Mr. Bossett's pictures and 1948, apparently removed altogether.

While visible, the coast artillery provided yet another among a growing list of reasons for tourists to visit Sea Girt. As the nineteenth century ended, annual National Guard encampments, featuring the governor's visit to review the troops, became an attraction at least equal to Salt Water Day. Governor Abbett's first review of the Guard at Sea Girt, on August 21, 1885, drew "thousands of people assembled from the Summer resorts near here and from inland villages to view the spectacle." By 1890, visitors "came in swarms from all parts of the country" to watch parades at Camp Abbett, and "a hundred handsome carriages containing elegantly attired ladies lined the road" as the troops marched by. There were so many civilians present at an 1893 review that it "was interfered with to some extent by crowds of visitors encroaching on the drill grounds." By 1896, a regular army lieutenant assigned to inspect the Sea Girt encampment complained about civilians being "allowed free access to the camp at all times," commenting that "the overrunning of camp by civilians is the cause of serious confusion."[76]

Rodman guns, 1916. *Courtesy New Jersey State Archives.*

Despite the lieutenant's concern, confusion continued into the next century, as annual summer training took on the aspects of a festive event or even carnival when the men were not actually drilling or shooting, much, no doubt, to the Quaker Mr. Morris's dismay. The camp itself continued to be deluged with visitors, and one soldier became a self-appointed guide for "a group of Spring Lake ladies…on a tour of inspection." Although one reporter claimed in 1901 that most men were in camp for serious reasons, providing they survived the "Squan skeeters" that appeared with a land breeze, he admitted that some soldiers were slipping past the guards and "skylarking" in neighboring resort towns at night. In the summer of 1904 a platoon of Trenton National Guardsmen crashed the gate of a circus performing in Manasquan. While some soldiers snuck off on unauthorized visits to Long Branch and Asbury Park, others held nightly mock Indian "War Dances" and "burlesques." "Blanket parties" and "watermelon parties," the latter ending in barrages of rinds, were commonplace. Unwanted guests also seemed able to penetrate camp security with little trouble, although Guardsmen finally captured a group of "tramps and camp hangers-on" who had "been giving the guards trouble for several days" in 1904 and hauled them off to Manasquan, where they were jailed.[77]

Serious business was conducted by the sea as well, however. Governor Abbett established his summer government headquarters in Sea Girt and the custom endured, with cabinet members, politicians, upper-level bureaucrats and judges in town for meetings. The newspapers dubbed Sea Girt New Jersey's "summer capital by the sea." In 1893, Governor George T. Werts and his family had already been living in the white frame farmhouse on the property for several weeks, "enjoying the fine air and beautiful environment," when the first National Guard troops arrived. As the Guard took over the camp, Werts moved his family to the Monmouth Hotel in Spring Lake, but continued to hold cabinet meetings on the campgrounds. Cabinet officers and other officials either moved to summer residences in nearby towns, including Belmar and Long Branch, or "took up rooms" at one of the Sea Girt or Spring Lake hotels.[78]

During the last decade of the nineteenth century and the first of the twentieth, the rifle ranges at Sea Girt were constantly improved. In addition to becoming a marksmanship training showplace for the New Jersey National Guard, Sea Girt also became a venue for a number of important civilian rifle matches. In 1894, the New Jersey Rifle Association opened a headquarters building on the range and hosted seven other states during its annual September competition week. New Jersey Guardsmen who trained at Sea Girt represented the state in national and international shooting contests, and in 1901 the range hosted the combined competitions of the National Rifle Association of America, the United States Revolver Association and the New Jersey State Rifle Association, as well as the Palma International Match between the United States and Canada and a match between the New Jersey State Rifle Association and the Ulster Rifle Association based in Belfast, Ireland. The United States team that won the 1903 Palma trophy in England practiced at the Sea Girt range. Sea Girt was the scene of the annual United States National Rifle Match in 1903, 1905 and 1906, when the competition outgrew available space and moved to a new home in Camp Perry, Ohio, where it is an annual event to this day.[79]

Sea Girt rifle range, 1905. *Courtesy Randy Gabrielan.*

For a brief time it appeared that the Sea Girt shooters might well be involved in a shooting war. Following the April 25, 1898 United States declaration of war on Spain, Secretary of War Russell A. Alger requested that New Jersey raise three regiments of volunteer infantry, to which a request for a fourth regiment was subsequently added. Acting Governor Foster M. Voorhees's attempts to augment that force by proposing two cavalry troops and two artillery batteries for federal service were rejected by the War Department. Anticipating an expansion of the Sea Girt facility, Voorhees negotiated with local property owners on the possibility of leasing their land. Companies from the First, Second, Third, Sixth and Seventh Regiments of the National Guard were ordered to Sea Girt to organize war service regiments. The units were mostly, but not exclusively, staffed by National Guard volunteers, as Guardsmen were given precedence in filling slots in the new outfits. Many years had passed since the country was last at war, and dim memories of its realities stoked enthusiasm. Some men who declined to volunteer for active service were pelted with mud balls by other soldiers as a penalty for their reluctance. The first company of the First New Jersey Volunteer Regiment was mustered into federal service at Sea Girt on May 6 and the last company of the Fourth Regiment on July 19, 1898. The war ended on August 12. No New Jersey regiments ever deployed overseas or faced the enemy, and all were mustered out of service by February 11, 1899.[80]

As a new century brought international prominence and worldwide responsibilities for the United States, Sea Girt assumed a new eminence in New Jersey's political and military affairs. The little town hosted its first presidential visit and mass political event when Theodore Roosevelt came to the National Guard Camp on July 24, 1902, to attend a reception and troop review hosted by New Jersey Governor and fellow Republican Franklin Murphy. Roosevelt landed at Highlands from his yacht and proceeded south on a train, with cheering, flag waving "Summer-clad" crowds greeting him at stations along the way. People placed coins on the tracks to be flattened by the president's car and used for watch fob souvenirs. The wildly popular "TR" was warmly welcomed as a crowd of "10,000 persons assembled along the parade field and prominent society folks from the resorts along the coast drove down in wagons, which lined the driveways." With the exception of brief scuffles between National Guardsmen and secret service officers in the press of people swarming toward the president, the visit went well. Roosevelt reviewed and then addressed the assembled Guardsmen, promising federal assistance in modernizing their weapons and equipment and, unsurprisingly, considering his reputation as a soldier and outdoorsman, stressing the importance of rifle marksmanship.[81]

Roosevelt's visit graphically demonstrated that the National Guard camp facilities for entertaining and housing the governor, his entourage and distinguished guests were severely limited, and the quartermaster general concluded that "a new headquarters house for the accommodation of the Governor and staff is urgently recommended." The rambling two-story farmhouse that stood on the property when the state acquired it, dubbed the "Little White House" by the press, was clearly inadequate. There was no doubt that something grander in the way of a residence for receiving dignitaries was needed, and state officials found it in the New Jersey Exhibit Hall at the 1904 Louisiana Purchase Exposition, popularly known as the Saint Louis World's Fair. The exposition, the most spectacular on record to that date, included exhibits from America's new overseas empire and served as a venue for the 1904 Olympic Games, the first conducted in the United States. Less significant exposition innovation claims included the introduction of the ice cream cone and, some say, the first hot dog and hamburger sales, although the latter two "firsts" are considered somewhat suspect.[82]

With the end of the Saint Louis extravaganza, the New Jersey hall, modeled on the Ford Mansion, General George Washington's Morristown headquarters during the winter of 1779–80, was disassembled and brought to Sea Girt, where it was reassembled in 1906. Described by the press as "a Colonial cottage, a century and a half old in design," the fifteen-room house was actually quite luxurious and modern on the inside, with three bathrooms, electric lighting and fancy furniture. It immediately inherited the "Little White House" nickname of its humble predecessor. Republican Governor Edward C. Stokes, the first summer occupant of the "cottage," moved in on July 7, 1906, for a month's stay, signaling the beginning of a new era for Sea Girt. In succeeding years, the state's governors would stretch their Sea Girt season to an entire summer,

Original Little White House in the 1890s. *Courtesy NGMMNJ.*

First Little White House (left) and successor, circa 1910. *Courtesy NGMMNJ.*

full of political and personal entertaining and deal making. Theodore Roosevelt's appearance proved the first of many Sea Girt national political celebrity sightings. Over the next three decades, a parade of state and national leaders made Sea Girt a must-stop on the campaign trail, and for forty years after the Roosevelt visit, the loyal and curious among the general public would flock to the little Monmouth County town by the sea in incredible numbers to see them.[83]

CHAPTER 4

Center of a Political Universe

As the nineteenth century closed, Sea Girt, although still relatively unpopulated, was gaining cachet as a resort. Informing a friend that his beachfront "cottage" was available for a $900 summer rental, Elliston Morris described the house as "3 stories high in front and four in rear and has 12 rooms." He went on to add that "all household supplies can be obtained without going beyond back gate. Grocery man calls twice a day, milk man, vegetable dealer & butcher every day." According to Morris, the town was now very accessible, and not only by railroad, since "good hard roads connect Sea Girt with Point Pleasant, Bay Head, Spring Lake, Como, Belmar, Asbury Park and Long Branch." Morris acquired telephone service to his cottage from the New York and New Jersey Telephone Company in 1903. Living was good in Sea Girt at the turn of the century, but there is no record of what Morris, whose struggle to keep his vacation property exclusive was lifelong, thought of the colony of summer tenters that grew up at Camp Cedar along the shore of Wreck Pond at the north end of town. Even though they were fairly far away from his "cottage," the camp's tents and one-room bungalows could not have made him happy.[84]

A few years later, Morris could have added trolley cars to his means of easy access to Sea Girt. The coastal trolley system, proposed in 1887 as an Asbury Park horse-drawn "street railway," quickly morphed into an electrified system with overhead wires supplying power. In ensuing years the street railroad system pushed south along the coast in fits and starts, as separate companies were formed, went bankrupt, merged and fought legal battles with local municipalities and Monmouth County. Despite these diversions, the trolley system, eventually consolidated as the Atlantic Coast Electric Railway, reached Sea Girt by the spring of 1905. The route crossed Wreck Pond and then ran down Fifth Avenue to Beacon Boulevard, east on Beacon to Third Avenue, down Third to Boston Boulevard and west on Boston to Sixth Avenue and the railroad station, where it was blocked from further progress by the tracks of the New York and Long Branch Railroad, which viewed trolleys as unwelcome competition. In 1906, Governor Stokes authorized the trolley company to negotiate with the state on a route south across the National Guard camp. It was 1912, however, before authorization was granted. Although the company requested permission from Wall Township and Manasquan to push farther south, construction never occurred, and the tracks across the camp to the

St. Uriel's Episcopal Church, Sea Girt, circa 1920. *Courtesy Randy Gabrielan.*

Manasquan border, completed in July 1913, were the last ever laid by the coastal trolley system. Street railways began a downward spiral in the automobile age that followed World War I. Privately owned vehicles and buses replaced trolleys, and a business that began with high hopes was, as many before and since, overwhelmed by technological change. Trolley service to Sea Girt ended on June 30, 1928.[85]

There were other marks of continuing progress, however, and Sea Girt even got its own lighthouse in 1896, erected just south of Wreck Pond. The location might seem an ironically appropriate place to establish a lighthouse, except for the fact that that body of water, sometimes referred to as Sea Girt Inlet, or Rack or Wrack Pond, was actually named after an old English word for seaweed, not in commemoration of shipwrecks, although it is a matter of record that the Jersey coast had more than its share of such wrecks. Nearby Manasquan inlet, when not silted up, was generally considered a safe haven in a storm.

Like the artillery on the beach, the lighthouse was a while in coming to town. It had its origins in the federal lighthouse board's annual report for 1888 assessing the thirty-eight-mile gap in the New Jersey lighthouse chain between Barnegat Inlet and Navesink Highlands. The report noted that "in view of the immense quantity of commerce passing both ways in this vicinity, this dark space should be lighted…it is therefore recommended that a light be established at or near a point about midway between Barnegat and Navesink light stations." A $20,000 Congressional appropriation to build a lighthouse followed. The original site was planned for Manasquan, but after several studies, disagreements and delays, Sea Girt was determined to be a better location, and construction began at Wreck Pond in 1896.[86]

Wreck Pond, circa 1910. *Courtesy Randy Gabrielan.*

Sea Girt beachfront, circa 1910. The lighthouse is to the right and Tremont House is on the left. *Courtesy Sea Girt Lighthouse.*

The lighthouse was equipped with a four-sided, beehive-shaped, fourth-order Fresnel lens, which had "two adjoining sides with rows of prisms surrounding bulls-eyes, the circular panes of glass at the center." Two brass doors gave access to the interior. The original red light, visible up to fifteen miles out at sea, was fired by a kerosene wick lamp. In 1912, an oil vapor lamp replaced the kerosene lamp and the lens chimney was changed from red to clear glass to provide a brighter light. In 1924, a 300-watt electric lamp was installed, dramatically increasing the light's luminescence from 11,000 to 100,000 candlepower. The Sea Girt lighthouse was not constructed in the classic free-standing tower configuration, but built as a brick structure with the keeper's house sort of wrapped around it. The first keeper, Civil War veteran Major Abraham Wolf, was paid $1.10 a day. When his successor, Abram Yates, died on the job in 1910, Yates's wife Harriet took over the keeper's duties and fulfilled them with distinction. After two months, however, she was replaced, as the lighthouse service had no provision for female keepers.[87]

Major Wolf, lighthouse keeper. *Courtesy Sea Girt Lighthouse.*

In the summer of 1907, some New York real estate investors organized as the Sea Girt Company, with Asbury Park attorney Frank Durand acting as "resident director," bought out the Pennsylvanians of the almost moribund Sea Girt Land Improvement Company. As part of the deal, the New Yorkers acquired the Tremont Hotel and a share in the Beach House, although the latter property was quickly resold. The Sea Girt Company established headquarters at 115 Broadway, New York City, bought advertising space in the *New York Times*—which proclaimed, "When summer comes again and you are weary of crowds and hustle, what a comfort it would be to go to your own Summer home at Sea Girt"—and produced a flashy brochure to promote its new property.[88]

The company accurately cited Sea Girt as "the Summer Capital of New Jersey," and touted its setting as "naturally the most beautiful spot on the Atlantic Coast, possessing every advantage and an ideal climate for summer or winter homes." Even the Sea Girt Land Improvement Company's failure to sell lots in the town was advertised as a plus, drawing praise as the calculated beneficent act of "a syndicate of wealthy Philadelphia gentlemen, who have allowed the greater part of it to remain in a practically undeveloped condition, so that now the Sea Girt Company has been able to purchase this magnificent property, unspoiled." The new company advertised lots of different sizes so that "some localities will be restricted to large plots and fine houses, while in others one may build

Frank Durand in 1937. *Courtesy of the author.*

on as few as two lots a bungalow or cottage of modest cost." Only "large hotels" were permitted to sell intoxicants, and no businesses were allowed in town except the hotels. No "stables or enclosures for chickens" were allowed "within 100 feet of the street," and no chickens were "allowed at large." The keeping of "swine" was forbidden in any form on any town property.[89]

Unlike in the 1880s, when its presence was protested and the conduct of its occupants criticized, the National Guard camp was now extolled as a positive community asset. According to the Sea Girt Company's literature, New Jersey's military training venue "speaks volumes for Sea Girt, as the State military authorities are very critical." No longer annoying drunks raising summer hell, "the soldier boys, many of whom are of the best families of New Jersey, are royally entertained, and the closing event, the Governor's Ball, is always a brilliant social event." The New Jersey and National Rifle Associations' marksmanship contests were also viewed as a plus, with the shooters described as "prominent men who usually bring their families to Sea Girt with them [and] their presence usually marks the height of the season here."[90]

Real estate sales picked up under the dynamic leadership of the New Yorkers. In 1899, Sea Girt gained its own post office, with postmistress Mary A. Blakey in charge, and by 1922 there were "about 200 dwellings" in town. Progress also brought unforeseen problems for the Sea Girt Company, however. By 1914 there were enough property owners to contest the community's dominance by the company, which claimed ownership of the streets, sewers and other public facilities even after selling the building lots. Some residents wanted the old Sea Girt Land Improvement Company alternate street plan that cut through Crescent Park implemented, and were frustrated to learn that the 1884 permanent injunction against disturbing the park was still in place. Disputes with the Sea Girt Company led Philadelphian J. Bunford Samuel to propose a merger with the neighboring municipality of Spring Lake, a flirtation that had been raised previously. Samuel believed that he and other "old property owners" were being slighted by the Sea Girt Company, and stated that company President Charles Noble told him he had "no intentions of aiding the old property owners." Spring Lake Mayor Oliver H. Brown, however, only seemed interested in accessioning the northern acreage of Sea Girt around Wreck Pond.

Although the proposed merger failed to materialize, it did hasten the push for a Sea Girt municipal government. In February 1917 residents of the town made formal application to the state for permission to incorporate as a borough. The application was approved on March 29 and elections for Sea Girt's first mayor and council were held on June 26. An organizational meeting by the successful candidates, headed by Mayor Charles E. Emerick, was held on July 2. A fire company was immediately formed and bought its first truck, a "Ford body with a Watrous pump," the following year, with a significant part of the cost donated by Mr. Samuel, who also put up $18,000 to build a borough hall, which stands to this day. Charles W. Roberts was appointed "town marshal" in 1917, and was succeeded by a "watchman" in 1925. A two-man formal police department was established in 1931. There was no more talk of merging with Spring Lake, although Sea Girt and Spring Lake residents did cooperate in establishing

Sea Girt Borough Hall, circa 1920. *Courtesy Sea Girt Lighthouse.*

Sea Girt Post Office, circa 1910. *Courtesy Randy Gabrielan.*

Sea Girt and Spring Lake Country Club horse show, circa 1920. *Courtesy Randy Gabrielan.*

Sea Girt Borough Hall, 2008. *Courtesy of the author.*

the privately owned Spring Lake and Sea Girt Country Club in 1908. The club, with a racetrack and steeplechase course, site of horse shows and polo matches, was actually located across the borough boundary in Wall Township, and was broken up for sale as building lots in the 1920s.[91]

The inevitable political squabbles of representative government were not long in raising their heads in the new borough. There was little opposition to jetty building to bolster an eroding shoreline, although responsibility for financing such work, and the best construction parameters to use, occasioned some confusion and dispute, and some private efforts gave less than satisfactory results. A bathing pavilion built on the beach in 1925 elicited no significant opposition, but one of the most contentious internal Sea Girt arguments in the early years of the borough became the building of a boardwalk along the beach, first proposed in the late 1920s. Charles M. Duncan, president of the Sea Girt Civic Association, claimed that 85 percent of respondents to his 1927 survey opposed boardwalk construction, and Duncan urged his members to attend a town council meeting to oppose the pro-boardwalk forces of Mr. Samuel and his Sea Girt Village Improvement Association. In the end, however, the project was approved by the borough council, which appropriated $40,000 to build a sixteen-foot-wide boardwalk along the town's oceanfront from Beacon Boulevard to Trenton Boulevard. The decision was ratified by a referendum of Sea Girt voters in November 1929. Beachfront property owners located on the ocean side of Crescent Park, including the litigious Morris family, now headed by Elliston's son Marriott C. Morris, opposed the project in the courts as violating their property rights, claiming it blocked their unfettered view of the sea. Their lawsuit was unsuccessful and the boardwalk was built.[92]

A far more serious squabble occurred in the summer of 1913, and Wall Township Special Officer Charles Roberts found the results on the morning of July 29 when he discovered a dead body sprawled under a tree across the road from the Little White House just outside the National Guard camp. The deceased, a short, heavyset man dressed in a blue suit, had three bullet holes in him and a knife wound on his hand. He was identified as George K. Harris by an envelope in his pocket. Harris, who claimed to be from Danbury, Connecticut, had flashed a wad of cash at a Spring Lake hotel and was thought to be a professional gambler down to roll dice and play cards with the Guardsmen in camp that week. Suspects included a mysterious "foreigner" who may have been smoking opium in his Sea Girt House hotel room and disappeared from the scene; a couple who ran a "wheel of fortune" game in Asbury Park; and several unidentified soldiers, one of whom reportedly threatened a civilian with a bayonet at the train station. The troops in camp that week were Hudson County boys from the Fourth New Jersey Infantry, a tough crew it would not do to trifle with or cheat. In the end, a coroner's jury pronounced the death of Harris a murder, but it was never solved. And so Sea Girt's only homicide remains, to this day, an open case.[93]

In 1920 the Beach House Hotel, abandoned and perched precariously over an eroding shoreline, was purchased by Nora Stubbs and was moved inland 150 feet. The original additions were retained but greatly expanded and the central section, Stockton's old mansion, was replaced by a much larger, more modern structure. In honor of the

National Guard Training Center, looking north, 1926. *Courtesy Claudia Gannon/NGMMNJ.*

Jersey City National Guardsmen of the Fourth Regiment, 1905. *Courtesy Dennin/NGMMNJ.*

man whose former home was removed, the new/old hostelry was rechristened the Stockton Hotel when it reopened on August 21, 1921. Stubbs's advertising brochure claimed, among the many obvious attributes and advantages of Sea Girt, the "weekly receptions at the Governor's Summer home...enjoyable functions which bring to Sea Girt many of the most prominent in the State's political life." In praising the delights of the hotel beach, her literature recalled the "custom among the Delaware Indians to flock for one day of the summer to the Sea Girt shore where they bathed and feasted on baked clams." Dubious aboriginal history aside, Salt Water Day and its August tradition of overall-clad Monmouth County farmers splashing in the surf went unmentioned.[94]

As Sea Girt began to grow into a real town, it received a dose of positive national publicity with the selection of New Jersey Governor Woodrow Wilson as the 1912 Democratic nominee for president. Wilson's nomination brought House of Representatives Speaker James Beauchamp "Champ" Clark and 116 Democratic congressmen up from Washington to Sea Girt on July 20 to greet the candidate. The visit made national news, with an Illinois paper claiming Clark's pilgrimage was "the first time in the history of the United States that a body of congressmen had quit their work to make a trip to hail the party standard bearer." Lower-ranking Democrats and curious members of the public flocked to Sea Girt as well, by train, trolley and automobile, to catch a glimpse of the candidate. One wag proposed a version of Big Sea Day to be known as Wilson Old Home Day, on which thousands of Democrats would camp on the National Guard parade ground and then jump fully clothed into the sea in Wilson's honor. In response to all of this attention, the nominee and his family fled the Little White House to a yacht in search of peace and quiet.[95]

The Stockton Hotel. *Courtesy Randy Gabrielan.*

Wilson, Virginia-born president of Princeton University, was talked into running for governor of New Jersey in 1910 by the state's Democratic Party bosses, but once in office championed the party's reform elements. His politics reflected a progressive tide building among both Republicans and Democrats in the early years of the twentieth century. Wilson's brief administration achieved some notable advances, including a workers' compensation program and electoral reform. These successes earned a national reputation that enabled him to secure the 1912 presidential nomination. Taking advantage of a Republican split, with Theodore Roosevelt running as a third-party candidate against both Wilson and Republican President William Howard Taft, the New Jersey governor won the presidency. The Sea Girt–trained New Jersey National Guard's elite Essex Troop of cavalry traveled down to Washington to provide an honor guard for the inaugural parade, but Wilson never returned to New Jersey's seaside summer capital.[96]

Wilson's successor, Governor James Fielder, continued the growing Sea Girt tradition as the state's summer headquarters by the sea. Fielder and his wife arrived in town in early June 1915, as a newspaper article reported that "Sea Girt always awaits the arrival of the State's chief executive and his wife before declaring the summer season open." The first event on the busy Little White House social agenda that year was a July 3 reception with an estimated attendance of 1,500 state officials and politicians of both parties.[97]

More grave business was afoot, however. Woodrow Wilson's presidency eventually brought Sea Girt to war. The Mexican Revolution of 1911 spilled over into the United States on March 9, 1916, when Revolutionary leader Pancho Villa raided Columbus, New Mexico, killing 14 American soldiers and 10 civilians. In response to Villa's incursion, the United States formed a "punitive expedition" under the command of Major General John J. Pershing. Wilson ordered 60 percent of the regular army to the Mexican border and called up 130,000 National Guardsmen to support the operation. On June 19, 1916, the New Jersey Guard assembled three infantry regiments, one cavalry squadron, two artillery batteries and their support companies at armories around the state and then proceeded to Sea Girt, to be mustered into federal service on June 26. The New Jersey units proceeded to Douglas, Arizona, by train. Pershing pushed deep into Mexico with a force of 12,000 regulars, but ultimately failed to kill or capture Villa. The army did, however, kill several Villista commanders (including one personally shot by First Lieutenant George C. Patton) and dispersed the Mexican rebel army. The Jerseyans never crossed the border or engaged in any combat, and returned to Sea Girt for demobilization in the fall of 1916.[98]

Despite the lack of action, the mobilization provided training for the National Guard's next big challenge. The Mexican border crisis, coupled with World War I in Europe, led to passage of a National Defense Act authorizing the call-up of Guardsmen for service as long as needed. German sabotage was a concern in New Jersey in light of the Black Tom island ammunition pier explosion of June 30, 1916, in Jersey City and the subsequent Kingsland detonation of January 11, 1917. With that in mind, Governor Walter E. Edge ordered a significant portion of the New Jersey Guard to active duty in

National Guardsmen in camp June 30, 1916, for Mexican border service. *Courtesy NGMMNJ.*

March 1917, before the April 6 declaration of war against Germany, to guard critical points within the state. Other Guardsmen were detailed to help build Camp Dix, the massive new army base in the New Jersey Pinelands. The remainder of the state's citizen soldiers were mobilized in July at Sea Girt's Camp Edge, named in honor of Governor Edge, who had served as a lieutenant in the Spanish-American war and a lieutenant colonel on Governor Franklin Murphy's staff following the war. The Jersey Guardsmen were soon on their way to Anniston, Alabama, where they, along with National Guard soldiers from Maryland, Virginia and the District of Columbia, were organized into the Twenty-ninth Division. The Twenty-ninth later fought in France in the Meuse-Argonne offensive. While the Guardsmen went to war, Governor Edge and the legislature created a state militia home guard to replace them. Camp Edge was closed following the departure of the New Jersey National Guard for Alabama, but reopened in 1918. Ten thousand state militiamen trained at Sea Girt that summer and the rifle range was also used by regular army soldiers. The ladies of Sea Girt pitched into the war effort as well, forming a Red Cross auxiliary that sent "baskets filled with clothing and edibles" for the troops overseas.[99]

At the end of World War I there were no active New Jersey National Guard units, since they had all ceased to exist when the Twenty-ninth Division was mustered out of service. Even after the end of active hostilities, the state militia continued to serve as New Jersey's military force and use Sea Girt for annual training. Military entertainment had become a staple at the annual encampment, and 1919 proved no exception. Newspaper advertisements advised the public to visit Sea Girt to see troop reviews and the aerobatics of "well known aviator Lieutenant Paul Micelli," who gave "an exhibition in fancy and acrobatic flying each day at 4:30" at the National Guard Camp. Micelli, a Jersey City native who had served in France with the American Field Service Ambulance Corps and later with the French and American air services in World War I, was a local celebrity

National Guardsmen's wives and sweethearts, summer of 1917. *Courtesy NGMMNJ.*

Aircraft at Camp Edge, 1916. *Courtesy Randy Gabrielan.*

and barnstormer. Unfortunately, one of his exhibitions at Sea Girt that year resulted in a crash on the parade ground that severely injured the pilot and killed his passenger, United States Navy Lieutenant R. Howard Monteith. Acting Governor William N. Runyon (Governor Edge had been elected to the U.S. Senate) was the first person on the scene and his car brought both men to the Spring Lake hospital. The fatal summer of 1919 was the final encampment for the state militia, which was disbanded on January 20, 1920. The National Guard began to reorganize from the bottom up that year and, as in the past, Sea Girt played a significant role in the process. Eventually the revitalized National Guard units, with new numerical designations reflecting their Twenty-ninth Division heritage, would be included in the new Forty-fourth Division, with its blue and orange insignia evoking the state's Dutch colonial heritage.[100]

The New Jersey Legislature approved $11,000 for maintenance of the Little White House and the governor's Sea Girt entertainment budget for the 1920 summer season. The camp reopened on June 6 as Camp Edwards, after new Democratic Governor Edward I. Edwards, for a series of instructional and reorganizational sessions for officers

Lieutenant Paul Micelli. *Courtesy Micelli file, NGMMNJ.*

and noncommissioned officers of the National Guard. General Spencer offered civilian riflemen free government ammunition for matches fired at Sea Girt to raise interest in the Guard's activities. Following the Edwards family's arrival, the press announced that Mrs. Edwards "will preside over the social activities which are being planned for the season at the executive mansion…[and] expressed her delight at the 'Little White House,'" which had been "decorated and refurnished."[101]

It would be a busy summer. In June 1920, Adjutant General Frederick Gilkyson moved his office to Sea Girt for the season. The Sixth New Jersey Infantry, commanded by Colonel Howard S. Borden, a wealthy socialite and polo player from Rumson who had served in the state militia during the war, encamped at Sea Girt in early July and "provided thousands of summer visitors with an insight into the highways and by-ways of military training." Borden's unit was followed by others from around the state. Daily parades and July 16 Governor's Day ceremonies before an assemblage of politicians from northern New Jersey provided entertainment for tourists and locals alike in a less sophisticated age. Government business was also conducted by the sea, and the New Jersey Court of Pardons convened to hear cases at the Little White House in July as well. The Sixth Infantry was followed into camp by the Third, along with cavalry and artillery units, and manager Mary McCarter of the Tremont Hotel sponsored a military ball for officers, with the Third Infantry band providing the music. Paul Micelli, recovered from his crash injuries and now a National Guard captain, returned to perform more exhibition flights, once again advertising for civilian thrill seekers who wanted to "see Spring Lake from the Air" or have an "aeroplane party."[102]

New York and Long Branch Railroad station, circa 1920. *Courtesy Randy Gabrielan.*

Aerial view, Sea Girt National Guard Training Center, circa 1930, looking south. *Courtesy Randy Gabrielan.*

In the following year, National Guard reorganization and recruiting picked up steam. During the winter, however, there was a serious flap when Colonel Borden was elevated to the rank of general in an election by officers thought to be currying favor with Governor Edwards. Other officers protested that Borden was a political hack and resigned their commissions. The feud lasted into the summer before a resolution was engineered by Edwards. The controversy seemed to have little effect on the lower ranks, however, and the Sea Girt location for summer training proved a prime recruiting tool. Potential new soldiers were encouraged to "join the National Guard" because "Uncle Sam offers you two weeks at the Seashore. All expenses paid. All equipment free." Recruits were not only guaranteed free room and board at the Jersey Shore, but advised that "Sea Girt offers ample opportunity for recreation and sport while the Guardsman is not on duty. There is swimming, boating and fishing, the site being in close proximity to many shore resorts."[103]

Some recruiters displayed more enthusiasm than judgment. When Private William Ryan's mother came to Sea Girt from Elizabeth to visit her soldier son in the summer of 1921, she discovered Willie confined to the guardhouse and "went home much upset." The following day, Ryan's father appeared with his son's birth certificate and declared that Willie was only fifteen years old, had been fraudulently enlisted in the National Guard and that his situation had exacerbated his mother's "heart trouble." The young man was promptly discharged. There was other excitement at Camp Edwards that summer, with the troops entertained by company boxing matches and baseball games (an outfielder was almost hit by a Curtiss biplane landing on the field) and YMCA

Guardsman at Sea Girt station, circa 1920. *Courtesy NGMMNJ.*

"movie performances." A review and tactical demonstration on July 17 drew ten thousand visitors.[104]

Despite the Guard officers' feud, the Sea Girt celebrity social calendar was full in the summer of 1921, with Governor Edwards playing his host role to the hilt. On July 22 the governor began his day with a horseback ride, "attired in riding togs. At noon he switched to a palm beach. Parade hour found the executive dolled up in frock coat and high hat. After reviewing the troops the governor changed to evening dress." Mrs. Edwards liked the high life as well, and Japanese servants reportedly "scampered about the executive mansion and grounds" at her beck and call. Senator Edge visited the governor, as did state legislators galore, and the air was full of rumors about future electoral politics. United States District Attorney Elmer Geran circled the camp in an airplane and State Police Commander Colonel Norman Schwartzkopf modeled that organization's new uniform. One observer remarked that he thought he was in Kentucky, with all the colonels walking about. The star of the summer, however, was General Pershing, who attended a reunion of World War I officers in Sea Girt that June. Edwards welcomed the gathering personally and provided them access to local recreational activities including shooting, fishing, baseball and swimming.[105]

Edward Irving Edwards, the genial and gracious Sea Girt host of 1920, was governor by virtue of his political alliance with Jersey City Mayor Frank Hague. He was Hague's first job placement outside Hudson County, and the first of a string of governors and senators who owed their positions to the tough Irish American urban political boss. Edwards won a close race in a year in which Republicans carried the day in every other Northern state. The nation elected Warren Harding president in an effort to "return to normalcy" following World War I and Woodrow Wilson's increasing unpopularity in a world seemingly turned upside down in the aftermath of the conflict, with revolutions abroad and a "Red Scare" at home. As the United States turned inward, the Republicans dominated national and many state elections throughout the 1920s. Hague and his protégés provided notable exceptions.

Frank Hague was a product of the "Horseshoe," a gerrymandered election district into which native-born Republican state legislators shoehorned Irish Catholic Democrats in 1871 to lessen their electoral power. Although the Republicans no doubt thought the Horseshoe (so called because of its shape on a map) a clever idea at the time, it would prove their undoing, for it produced a large number of angry underrepresented voters with scores to settle—and Frank Hague saw to it that they did. Born in a Horseshoe tenement in 1876, Hague came up the hard way. Expelled from elementary school, he ran the neighborhood with the Red Tigers street gang, worked odd jobs and was an unsuccessful prizefighter and manager before entering politics under the tutelage of local boss and saloonkeeper Ned Kenny.[106]

In 1899, Hague was elected constable and began his rapid rise in the world of Hudson County Democratic politics. Running as a Wilsonian-style reformer, he was elected public safety commissioner in 1913 and hired tough Irishmen from the Horseshoe to sweep pickpockets, muggers and prostitutes from the streets of Jersey City and close firetrap movie houses. Hague proved so effective that in 1917 he easily won election as mayor, an office he held for the next thirty years. His power base grew to include all of Hudson County, and he delivered enough votes to control most statewide races for the next two decades. Indeed, as often reported, the dead did vote Democrat in Hudson County, but Hague's amazing success was primarily the result of his ability to create and fund (from legal and illegal sources) the most efficient "get out the vote" political machine in American history. In 1910, seven of ten residents of Jersey City were either born abroad or had at least one foreign-born parent, and the majority of them were Catholics. A decade later the census reported that one out of every four New Jerseyans was an immigrant, with most living in the crowded cities of the state's northeast. "Duh Mare," as he was known in Jersey City-ese, became the champion of the immigrants against the state's native-born rural and small-town Republican majority. There were not enough Hague voters to take control of the New Jersey Legislature, which was based on county representation, but there were enough to dominate elections for governor and senator with regularity.[107]

Ironically, Frank Hague's governors and senators were members of the native-born Protestant majority who allied themselves with his organization and shared urban-friendly and anti-Prohibition attitudes with their unlikely constituency. Edwards, governor from 1920 to 1923, was a Hudson County businessman, bank president and former state comptroller and senator. His successor as governor, George S. Silzer, was a Middlesex County attorney and judge. The most notable Hagueite of the era, however, was A. Harry Moore. Under the 1844 Constitution then in place, a governor served a three-year term and could not succeed himself. Moore, a consistent winner for Hague when called on, was governor three times, serving from 1926 to 1929, 1932 to 1935 and 1938 to 1941. Both Edwards and Moore were also elected as United States senators. A. Harry Moore enjoyed his Sea Girt summers as much as he did his office, and spent more time in the town than any New Jersey politician before or since.[108]

In 1928, Frank Hague moved from the state to the national stage, and carried Sea Girt along with him. As vice chairman of the National Democratic Committee, he scheduled a Sea Girt visit by New York Governor Alfred E. Smith, the first Catholic nominated to run for president, and choreographed the trip from start to finish with the intent of making nationwide news. Hague guaranteed the press that his Sea Girt rally

Governor A. Harry Moore and military staff. *Courtesy New Jersey State Archives.*

for the nominee would "surpass any other political event ever held in this State or any other State in the Union." Smith's motorcade crossed into New Jersey via the Holland Tunnel, which he and Moore had officially opened the previous year, and proceeded south through the solidly Democratic towns of Jersey City, Newark and Elizabeth, cheered along the way by upward of 100,000 supporters. According to one account, "miles of factories turned out employees in shop clothes to greet him" and "steel and iron workers in black aprons and bare arms tossed their caps." The motorcade ended at Spring Lake, where 500 Democratic Party leaders greeted Governor Smith on the lawn of the Monmouth Hotel.[109]

That evening, Smith attended a ball at the Monmouth sponsored by Governor Moore, and arrived at Sea Girt the following afternoon. Frank Hague made sure a veritable sea of people was there to greet him. Bands played continuous rounds of "East Side, West Side" Manhattan and Smith's anthem, as National Guardsmen, New Jersey State Police and Jersey City Police on loan for the occasion escorted Smith into Camp Moore, fending off the press of people struggling for a close-up view of the candidate. The day provided another Sea Girt historic first, as New Jersey State Police aerial observers in biplanes assisted in controlling traffic for thirty miles around the town. The observers dropped messages attached to sandbags at locations in Sea Girt, Keyport, Farmingdale and Toms River, but apparently also communicated with airborne "radio and wireless telephones." Colonel Schwartzkopf was surprised and impressed by the results of the experiment, noting that "jams were kept to a minimum." Newspapers across the country carried the Al Smith story on their front pages, noting that Woodrow Wilson planned his own presidential campaign at Sea Girt's Little White House, a fact that hardly hurt the Democratic candidate. One paper called Smith's first personal appearance since his nomination "the greatest Democratic rally in the history of New Jersey." Other accounts described the gathering as "such a crowd as this state has never seen before," and the "greatest throng ever gathered in Jersey." Attendance estimates ranged from 80,000 to 200,000 people, with the lower number more likely. Frank Hague's formidable executive skills were much in evidence, as "more than fifty special trains…converged on Sea Girt, swelling the throng that arrived by automobile."[110]

Not everything went perfectly, however. One enthusiastic Smith supporter, John "Spike" Sullivan of Jersey City, "almost succeeded in shaking hands with the presidential candidate at Sea Girt," but was prevented from doing so by "a big cop about 7 foot tall and three feet wide." The combative Sullivan told a reporter that he "could have knocked him for a goal. I was that mad." The horse-drawn coach Moore and Smith rode in to review the troops nearly tipped over when a National Guardsman's mount spooked a carriage horse. And a few miles north of Sea Girt at the Ocean Grove Annual Camp Meeting, evangelist Billy Sunday railed against the Democratic candidate as a "Tammanyite, a Catholic and wet." Sunday assured his audience that Smith's election would be "a national calamity."[111]

It certainly didn't seem that way at Sea Girt. At the end of the day, special trains pulled out of town at precise ten-minute intervals, with amplifiers on poles connected to a dispatcher at a temporary tower announcing departures. The candidate was awed

Al Smith at Sea Girt, August 25, 1928. *Courtesy Micelli file, NGMMNJ.*

Governors A. Harry Moore, Al Smith and their wives, August 25, 1928. *Courtesy Micelli file, NGMMNJ.*

Governors Moore and Smith in the "Tally Ho" coach, August 25, 1928. *Courtesy Micelli file, NGMMNJ.*

by the whole operation, to be sure. At the end of the affair a newspaper account had Smith relaxing "on the veranda of the Little White House, contentedly puffing one of his big cigars," seeing "in the rings of smoke he blew a vision of himself in the Big White House in Washington." Hague seemed at the peak of his power, but within months the mayor's empire began an apparent downward spiral. Smith, in an uphill struggle against Republican-credited prosperity and the Billy Sundays of the country, lost his presidential bid to Herbert Hoover in a landslide that included New Jersey and carried Senator Edward I. Edwards down with him. Morgan Larson, who had ironically gained the Republican nomination for governor due to Hague's infiltration of the opposition's primary process, won the statehouse against Democrat William L. Dill, who he accused of "Hagueism." Although Hague was reelected, it was by his smallest majority ever. Despite his elevation to national status at Sea Girt, Frank Hague's popularity among rank and file Jersey City Democrats had begun to ebb when it became apparent he had a personal agenda of making as much money as possible out of his office. His anti-union stance during labor violence surrounding the building of the Pulaski Skyway—along with stories of government worker kickbacks, dubious real estate deals, cash-filled suitcases dispatched from city hall to New York stockbrokers and the "horse bourse" bookie consortium and other gambling enterprises operating under Hague's protection for a fee, coupled with a Republican governor able to appoint judges and prosecutors—made "Duh Mare's" days seem numbered.[112]

The Depression came to his rescue. By 1932, the national economic picture was so dismal it became apparent that whoever secured the Democratic nomination would win the presidential election. Al Smith wanted that nomination badly, and his friend Frank Hague served as his floor manager at the Democratic Convention, telling one and all that Smith's competitor, New York Governor Franklin D. Roosevelt, was unelectable. Once Roosevelt secured the party nod, however, Hague switched his loyalty, and to prove it promised Roosevelt's campaign manager James Farley that if FDR would hold

Biplane crash into the Little White House, June 1929. *Courtesy NGMMNJ.*

his first campaign event in New Jersey he would stage the biggest political rally in history for the candidate. Farley agreed, and the mayor went to work to exceed his achievement of four years earlier.[113]

Hague succeeded again—and this time it stuck. Governor Larson's policies had evoked strong opposition from his fellow Republicans as well as Democrats. The governor ended up being tagged, perhaps unfairly, but inevitably given the times, as a New Jersey clone of President Herbert Hoover, and was succeeded in office by A. Harry Moore. Aside from the large servants' quarters addition he tacked onto the Little White House, the most significant event of Larson's term may well have occurred when a joyriding airplane crashed into the residence's top floor in the summer of 1929.

With Governor Moore back in office, Sea Girt, which had become the preferred "rallying point for the New Jersey Democracy," was available once more, and the ensuing festivities on August 27, 1932, described in the press as "a traditional Hague rally," followed the Smith script. Roosevelt's motorcade was met at the Holland Tunnel's New Jersey exit by little girls bearing bouquets, and then proceeded south through cheering crowds lining the sidewalks of the state's Democratic-leaning urban heartland to Hague's summer home in Deal, where the mayor and candidate greeted each other and proceeded on to Sea Girt. While Moore, Hague, Roosevelt and other dignitaries lunched in the Little White House, a massive crowd assembled on the Camp Moore parade ground, entertained by fireworks, stunt planes flying overhead and vaudeville vocalists singing the candidate's campaign song, "Row, Row, Row with Roosevelt." Hague claimed a crowd of 200,000 to 250,000 in attendance, but the *New York Times*, which displayed a distinct lack of enthusiasm for the mayor, estimated the gathering as having "no more than 100,000 present." State Democratic Committee Chairman

Harry Heher of Trenton, who introduced Roosevelt, later recalled that "there must have been a hundred thousand people" present. One source maintains, however, that the crowd that day was "considerably more than a hundred thousand people." Although the 1932 multitude's mood, no doubt dampened by the deepening Depression, was not as rambunctious as that of its 1928 predecessor, FDR's attacks on Hoover and demand for repeal of Prohibition evoked "a long cheer." And so it was that Franklin D. Roosevelt began his inexorable climb to worldwide fame in Sea Girt, New Jersey.[114]

The FDR rally put Frank Hague back in business. Although Roosevelt personally disliked the Hudson County boss, he patronized him, well aware that Hague's machine could deliver enough votes to reliably put New Jersey in the Democratic electoral column in statewide and national elections. A Hague loyalist was appointed to supervise the distribution of the state's Works Progress Administration (WPA) Depression-fighting money and award the ninety-seven thousand jobs the program brought to New Jersey, and Governor Moore referred all WPA employment applicants to Hague's office. With the influx of federal funds, Hague built the A. Harry Moore School, Roosevelt Stadium and, most importantly to him, Jersey City Medical Center, a complex that still stands today in art deco splendor as the Beacon luxury condominiums, and where the people of Jersey City received quality medical care at little or no cost to themselves. As Hague grew older, however, he grew, to paraphrase the old Irish saying, "more like himself"—

The west wing addition to the Little White House. *Courtesy NGMMNJ.*

Above: The reception room of the Little White House, circa 1935. *Courtesy NGMMNJ.*

Left, left to right: Frank Hague, Franklin D. Roosevelt and A. Harry Moore in the Little White House, August 27, 1932. *Courtesy National Archives and Records Administration/FDR Library.*

FDR addresses crowd, August 27, 1932. *Courtesy National Archives and Records Administration/FDR Library.*

increasingly dictatorial and greedy. He wrangled with labor unions, opposed programs like Social Security that would replace him as a source of government benefits and continued to skim large amounts of money from municipal coffers. In 1947, political revolts simmering in the Hudson County Democratic Party, coupled with the election of reform-minded Republican Governor Alfred E. Driscoll and the adoption of a new state constitution giving more power to the executive, convinced Hague to retire. There have been American political bosses before him and after him, but none has ever equaled the power and skill of Frank Hague, who rose from humble birth in the Horseshoe in 1876 to die a millionaire in New York City in 1956, whose name became synonymous with the dark side of New Jersey politics and who brought Sea Girt onto the national stage.[115]

In September of 1934, however, Hague was still riding high. Despite the continuing pervasive and deep economic dislocation of the Depression, things were beginning to get back to normal on the New Jersey political front. It would be another year before the WPA was created, but the mayor was looking forward to federal money for Jersey City projects, secure in the knowledge that no one in Washington would look too closely at any cash skimmed off. A. Harry Moore was enjoying the waning days of summer at his favorite place, the Little White House at Sea Girt. And then, seemingly out of nowhere, disaster came at sea, and the governor, the National Guard and the people of Sea Girt were soon in the thick of it. Once more the little town, with some help with the Associated Press wire service, would make newspaper front pages nationwide.

The tragedy that brought Sea Girt back into the headlines was completely unforeseen. For four years the luxury ocean liner *Morro Castle* sailed past the Jersey coast several miles out at sea on its regular round trips to Cuba. Launched in 1930 for the express purpose of making a regular run back and forth to Havana and named for a fort overlooking that city's harbor, the *Morro Castle*, with a capacity of almost five hundred passengers and a crew half as large, was able to reach Cuba from New York in less than sixty hours. Despite the dark years of the Depression, the *Morro Castle* and its sister ship the *Oriente* were popular with a variety of people, including business travelers, tourists and, prior to the 1933 repeal of the Eighteenth Amendment to the Constitution and its enabling legislation, vacationers who, once beyond the three-mile limit, made the Caribbean trip an oceangoing drinking party.

On September 5, 1934, the *Morro Castle* left Havana on a seemingly routine return trip to New York under the command of Captain Robert Wilmott. As the ship approached New Jersey on September 7, it encountered the lashing wind and rain of a classic northeaster storm. That evening Wilmott complained he was not feeling well, took dinner in his quarters, went to bed and never woke up. When the captain's death from an apparent heart attack was discovered, Chief Officer William Warms took command of the ship and continued its course north through rising seas. At 3:00 a.m. on September 8, however, a fire was discovered aboard the *Morro Castle*, then somewhat south of Sea Girt, and within a half hour the ship was engulfed in flames. The conflagration spread rapidly for a number of reasons, including highly flammable wood finishes and a ventilation system intended to cool the ship's passengers in hot tropic seas, which, combined with high winds and ship speed, fanned the flames. The blaze destroyed the vessel's control systems and it began to drift toward the New Jersey beaches. Although he anchored his ship to await assistance some two miles off the coast, Warms's lack of leadership soon led to chaos aboard the doomed liner. Passengers and crew tried to launch lifeboats, but only half the available boats ended up in the water. Desperate passengers and crewmen, a few in life vests and others without, began to jump overboard into surging seas, where some grasped onto floating deck chairs tossed off the ship in desperation. As the fire spread, radio operator George Rogers stayed at his post sending out SOS pleas, and word of the catastrophe spread quickly up and down the Jersey coast and beyond.[116]

The *Morro Castle* tragedy would prove the finest hour of New Jerseyans as diverse as A. Harry Moore; the party fishing boat Bogan family; Jack Holthusen's Sea Girt lifeguard team; the African American soldiers of Companies A and B of the National Guard's segregated First Separate Battalion, in camp for their annual training stint; and the ordinary citizens of Sea Girt and neighboring communities. Moore, a late sleeper, was awakened at 8:30 on the stormy Saturday morning of September 8 by his wife Jennie. Mrs. Moore told the governor she had received a phone call about the developing disaster from his secretary, Frances Smith, who was staying at the Stockton Hotel. Moore immediately ordered Adjutant General William A. Higgins to make all National

Guard resources available to rescuers. The black Guardsmen were soon fanning out to patrol the beach from Point Pleasant to Belmar, on the lookout for survivors and bodies washing ashore. At the same time, Holthusen's lifeguards and the people of Sea Girt, Spring Lake and other coastal towns began to move to the beaches. Twelve-year-old Jack Geiger, whose family had sailed on the *Morro Castle* on a previous vacation voyage, awakened at 6:00 a.m. in his Spring Lake home to the news that there was a ship burning offshore and went down to the beach to join a growing crowd of local people looking out to sea. They could all see the *Morro Castle* on the horizon, glowing like a "globe of fire." And the desperate passengers could see the Sea Girt lighthouse, which gave them "direction and hope."[117]

Back at Camp Moore, the governor ordered Captain John A. Carr of the National Guard's 119th Observation Squadron to warm up his Douglas O-2H biplane. When Carr was ready to fly, the governor jumped into the observer's open rear seat. Carr took off from the Sea Girt camp's parade ground and flew out over the pounding surf into the storm, coursing back and forth between Point Pleasant and Asbury Park, "from close inshore to five or six miles out at sea," searching for survivors bobbing in the waves. By the time the governor's plane reached the burning cruise ship itself, rescue vessels had

Morro Castle lifeboat on Spring Lake beach, September 8, 1934. *Courtesy Sea Girt Lighthouse.*

appeared on the scene and let down lifeboats to pick up people in the water. Whenever Moore and Carr spotted a survivor, the governor stood up in his seat and waved a red flag to indicate the location, while Carr dropped smoke bombs to indicate the presence of floating dead bodies. The governor literally risked his life in high winds and seas, leaning out of his seat as the plane "circled and dipped" seventy-five to one hundred yards above the rolling waves. After an hour in the air, the O-2H flew back to Sea Girt, where Carr landed on the parade ground with only a pint of fuel left in his tank and Navy Commander Thomas Mulroy flew another National Guard plane out to sea to continue the search. Carr and Moore were emotionally and physically drained, the governor recalling later in the day, "I shall never forget what I saw."[118]

It was not a good morning to take the Bogan family's party fishing boat, the *Paramount*, to sea. The Bogans were working on the sixty-foot vessel, a former rumrunner bought at government auction, at the Brielle docks when they heard news of the disaster and contacted the Coast Guard station at Shark River offering to help. John Bogan and his sons, Jim and John Jr., were soon on their way out the Manasquan inlet with a volunteer crew. They hesitated a moment as a huge wave crested over the *Paramount*'s bow, and then John Jr. shouted, "We've got to go out there." And they did. The Bogans went to work immediately on arrival at the burning ship, pulling sixty-seven people to safety over a four-hour period. In the process, they almost lost John Bogan, who was nearly swept overboard by a wave as he straddled the rail dragging survivors onboard. Back at the dock later, John recalled that the "water seemed to be full of dead people," and the scene was the "most horrible sight I ever saw."

A hundred more passengers and crewmen landed on local beaches in lifeboats, some from the *Morro Castle* and others from rescue ships whose boats could not get back to them. Other survivors swam or floated in. Holthusen's team—including Tom Black, Elvin Lake, Dick Tucker, George Braender and Jack Little—tied a rope around their leader, the strongest swimmer, who crossed the breakers to grab survivors, and then pulled him back in against the powerful undertow. Mr. and Mrs. Abraham Cohen jumped from the *Morro Castle* deck hand in hand and holding a single life jacket and were eventually swept up on the Sea Girt beach. Citizens and first aid workers took the Cohens, lifeboat survivors and 15 people pulled out of the surf by the lifeguards to the Sea Girt police headquarters, where "women of the town quickly organized and started serving hot coffee and food to the men and women." Similar scenes played out in all the little towns along the southern Monmouth County coast. The disaster proved the first test for the men of the newly formed Manasquan first aid squad, who rushed to the rescue. When 155 survivors came ashore in lifeboats at Spring Lake, many citizens flocked to the first aid squad and fire department to help out. Forty years later, Spring Lake Police Officer Lewis Morris vividly recalled Mrs. George Washington Kavanaugh, "who marched around the cots in her big straw hat and straw bag with a bottle of whiskey and a carton of cigarettes, dispensing a drink and smoke to anyone who wanted it."[119]

News of the disaster spread quickly by radio, and by afternoon curiosity seekers from around the state were driving to the shore. Newspapers were, needless to say, a step behind with the story, but eager to catch up. John J. Farrell, executive editor of the

Crew of the *Paramount* who saved sixty-seven *Morro Castle* survivors. Captain Jim Bogan is fifth from left, flanked by brother John Jr. and father John Sr. *Courtesy Sea Girt Lighthouse.*

Sea Girt lifeguards who rescued *Morro Castle* survivors. *Left to right*: Jack Holthusen, Tom Black, Elvin Lake, Dick Tucker, George Brender and Jack Little. *Courtesy Sea Girt Lighthouse.*

Newark News, who was ending a Sea Girt summer with his family, spotted a young man taking pictures, bought his camera and undeveloped film on the spot, jumped in his car and headed north to Newark with it. By early evening, relatives of passengers began to appear, seeking word of their loved ones. They would find some of them at the National Guard Camp. Soldiers from the First Separate Battalion who were morticians in civilian life established a temporary morgue at the camp under the supervision of Colonel Eugene H. Vallee, who requested that all bodies be transported there for identification. Fifty-seven were brought in from the Coast Guard station at Manasquan, thirty-two from Point Pleasant and another twenty-eight from the Sea Girt beach. The deceased were lined up on cots and covered with white sheets in a building variously described as a "barracks," "Post Exchange" or "dining hall." Anxious relatives soon appeared to identify the dead and were guided through the room by soldiers, with nurses on hand for support. When one man was overcome by grief on finding his younger brother among the dead, a reporter noted that "a Negro militiaman, a guard with a rifle on his shoulder, left his post to comfort him, and to guide him to a secluded place where he might have an undisturbed rendezvous with grief." Some relatives claimed their loved ones at Sea Girt, and on September 10, remaining bodies were removed to Jersey City by train.[120]

In the end, 135 of the 549 passengers and crew onboard the *Morro Castle* that day died, and then the ill-fated vessel broke loose from a towing ship and drifted into the

Morro Castle survivors at Brielle docks. Ike Norris of Spring Lake is on the right in white clothing. *Courtesy Bud Norris.*

beach at Asbury Park, where flimflam men and grifters were soon charging admission to journalists and the curious. A nineteenth-century Asbury Park newspaperman had once posited that the town needed "a first-class shipwreck" to boost tourism. Now it had it. Signs directing the curious to the still smoldering hulk appeared almost instantly on nearby roads, and as many as 100,000 tragedy tourists flocked to the beach over the next few days. Saltwater taffy and popcorn sales boomed and *Morro Castle* postcards appeared on the boardwalk soon afterward. Some members of the Asbury Park City Council, seeing a way out of the town's Depression doldrums, tried to negotiate a purchase of the ship for a permanent tourist attraction, but backed off when Councilman Max Silverstein called the idea "shocking" and "revolting." The novelty wore off after a while, especially when the *Morro Castle*'s below decks' cargo of animal hides began to rot and the stench wafted over the beach. The merchants and politicians of Asbury Park were not sorry to see the rusty wreck finally go when it was towed off for scrap on March 14, 1935. In November, A. Harry Moore was elected to the United States Senate, taking office in January 1935. Senate Bill 1874, proposing a commendation to the Sea Girt lifeguards, the Bogans and A. Harry Moore (Moore recused himself from voting) was introduced that year, but failed to pass when the larger law to which it was attached was filibustered.[121]

After all the excitement of politics and disaster in the first half of the decade, the rest of the 1930s passed quietly in Sea Girt. When Senator Moore went to Washington, Harold G. Hoffman came to Trenton as the state's new governor. The South Amboy–

Morro Castle, Asbury Park beach. *Courtesy Bud Norris.*

Above: Morro Castle casualties on Brielle dock. *Courtesy Bud Norris.*

Left: The *Morro Castle* fire on Asbury Park beach. *Courtesy NGMMNJ.*

born executive was a rare Republican who bucked the Democratic electoral tide of the mid-1930s. Hoffman, a New Jersey National Guard World War I hero who earned a promotion to captain on the Meuse-Argonne battlefield in 1918, became a bank officer after the war and served as an assemblyman, mayor, congressman and New Jersey Motor Vehicle commissioner before running for governor. An excellent and charismatic campaigner able to siphon off Democrat votes, Hoffman, a well-known and popular figure in the state at the time of the election, pulled off an upset over his colorless opponent, Frank Hague protégé Judge William L. Dill.[122]

Unfortunately for him, Hoffman's election proved the high point of his administration. The governor's failed attempt to enact a sales tax to better fund state government gained him the enmity of many in his party and an ironic alliance with Hague and other big city politicians. An intervention in the case of convicted Lindbergh kidnapper Bruno Hauptman proved another disaster. Despite these missteps Hoffman, a relentless self-promoter with higher ambitions, maneuvered for a vice-presidential slot on the Republican national ticket. His ability to attract Democratic voters actually gained him some support, but his hopes crashed when he barely secured a place among the state's

Governor Harold Hoffman and wife at the Monmouth County Country Club in 1937. *Courtesy of the author.*

convention delegates. A combative character who apparently believed that any press, even unfavorable, was good press, Hoffman constantly wrangled with reporters and actually engaged in fistfights with two of them during his term.[123]

The governor seemed to generate trouble of varying degrees wherever he went, even during his Sea Girt summers. Hoffman requested a parade ground parachute jump as part of the 1935 Governor's Day festivities, but participant Albert Ulrich drifted away from the Camp Hoffman drop zone and crashed through a window of Edward K. Whitmore's Sea Girt home. The governor paid three dollars to replace Mr. Whitmore's glass. A more serious incident occurred in the summer of 1937, when Hoffman went fishing on his thirty-two-foot yacht. While the governor was joking with crewmen who had attached a bucket to his line to fool him into thinking he had hooked a big fish, the boat's engine suddenly exploded. Unfazed, Hoffman displayed the cool that had earned him promotion under fire in France two decades earlier, refusing to leave the sinking craft until everyone else onboard, including his wife and two daughters, were safely aboard a Coast Guard rescue vessel. As befitting the commander in chief of the New Jersey National Guard—and the only combat veteran to hold that position since Civil War veteran Franklin Murphy left office in 1905—Hoffman took his military duties seriously, sitting astride a horse at Sea Girt's daily National Guard retreat ceremonies, which were much attended by local children who bicycled over to the camp to listen to the band and watch the troops march by. At the end of a long day, the governor could refresh himself by stepping into the special shower with ten separate showerheads he had installed in the Little White House.[124]

Despite political and personal travails, Governor Hoffman often personally intervened in assisting people in need. He saw to it that partially paralyzed Winifred Menke of Neptune received state-of-the-art treatment from a Hasbrouck Heights doctor who cured her. Winifred later appeared as guest of honor at a "crippled children's party" thrown by Hoffman at the Sea Girt Little White House. He was loyal to old friends and army buddies like William A. Hill, keeping in touch by letter, telegram and invitations to Governor's Day receptions at the Little White House. The colorful governor was a much-requested after-dinner speaker and a toastmaster of the Order of Circus Saints and Sinners, a charitable association dedicated to assisting down and out circus performers. Unfortunately for his legacy, which would have been mixed at best, in 1954 evidence surfaced that Hoffman, then New Jersey employment security director, had embezzled at least $300,000 from the state coffers during his long career to offset other money he purloined from his Perth Amboy bank. Before he could be indicted, he died of a heart attack, leaving a full confession in a last letter to his daughter.[125] .

Throughout all the political hoopla of the 1930s, the New Jersey National Guard continued to conduct annual summer training at Sea Girt. The training often spilled over into the surrounding countryside. Longtime Wall Township resident Jack Hendrickson, who was living on his grandfather's farm on Gully Road in Wall as a child in the 1930s, recalls seeing the Guard's 102nd Cavalry Regiment marching west in a seemingly endless line of horsemen along Belmar Boulevard, then a dirt road, troopers tossing candy to children running along in their wake. The cavalrymen dismounted

Above: Little White House back porch, circa 1935. *Courtesy NGMMNJ.*

Right: Governor Harold Hoffman's war buddy, William A. Hill (center). *Courtesy Ted Hill.*

and tied their mounts along the fence line in front of the farm, where the Tower Lodge Nursing Home now stands. On one occasion, Hendrickson recalls, a horse kicked a nest of "ground hornets" and they swarmed out, stinging animals and soldiers alike, creating temporary chaos. Such innocent rural maneuvers would soon give way to more serious military business.[126]

By the time Harold Hoffman's term began to wind down, Senator A. Harry Moore, no doubt missing his Sea Girt summers, had tired of Washington, and when the opportunity presented itself, he successfully ran again for governor in 1937. On September 1, 1939, during Moore's third and final term in the statehouse, and his next to last Sea Girt seasonal sojourn, the German army invaded Poland, igniting World War II and leading to events that would transform the world, the United States, New Jersey and Sea Girt forever.

CHAPTER 5
Goodbye to All That

By midsummer 1940, the Germans had overrun Western Europe and were mercilessly bombing Great Britain. On August 27, Congress declared a state of national emergency and authorized President Roosevelt to federalize the National Guard for a period of one year, stipulating that the Guardsmen not be deployed outside of the Western Hemisphere except in American overseas possessions. On August 31, the men of the New Jersey National Guard's 44th Division, less the 44th Tank Company, 119th Observation Squadron and 102nd Cavalry, were ordered to report for active duty by September 16, the same day Roosevelt signed a bill authorizing the first peacetime draft in the nation's history.[127]

A. Harry Moore, his retirement from a long and productive political life a few months away, instructed the state's soldiers to assemble at their armories for mobilization. In what would be his farewell message to the Guard and Sea Girt, Moore expressed gratitude to the Guardsmen, praising them as "inheritors of [a] proud tradition of preparedness and sacrifice," and noting that "as one who has often visited your armories and encampments and who has, in a sense, lived with you for several years in your camp at Sea Girt, I wish you well." By January, the remaining Guard units were all in federal service.[128]

As war crept closer to America, Frank Hague had one more act to play out at Sea Girt. The Democratic candidate to succeed Moore was Charles Edison, son of inventor and entrepreneur Thomas Edison. The younger Edison, a successful businessman who ran his father's company and dabbled in poetry and songwriting, was secretary of the navy in Roosevelt's cabinet when, encouraged by the president, he decided to run for governor of New Jersey. No Democrat seeking statewide office could win or even run without the approval and support of Hague. The boss gave Edison his blessing, however, and, of equal importance, a Hague-style Sea Girt rally.[129]

Hague outdid himself for Edison on August 24, 1940, at Sea Girt, even according to the *New York Times*, which reported that "never was the showmanship of Mayor Frank Hague of Jersey City so manifest as in the day's outpouring of a crowd estimated at 150,000 to 200,000." Although the music and fireworks of days past seem to have been lacking, the *Times* added that "the event outshone even its two notable predecessors, the Smith and Roosevelt days of 1928 and 1932, neither of which attracted so vast an assemblage of

Sea Girt View Hotel and Grill, 1939. *Courtesy Randy Gabrielan.*

Back porch of the Little White House, circa 1935. *Courtesy NGMMNJ.*

Governor Charles Edison. *Courtesy New Jersey State Archives.*

Democrats." Hague's multitude arrived at Sea Girt on "more than sixty special trains, forty-seven of which came from North Jersey counties, by scores of specially chartered busses from every section of the state, and in thousands of privately owned cars." The huge rally spilled out of the National Guard camp, and "nearby beaches were peppered with thousands who went there for recreation and to eat their boxed luncheons." Hague was prepared for everything, and first aid stations were established "at numerous points on the State reservation and in the outlying streets. First aid squads were busy all day removing ailing persons from the vast crowds and administering to them at the stations where trained nurses and doctors were on duty."[130]

Had Frank Hague listened closely to what Charles Edison said that day at Sea Girt, he might have been alarmed. The candidate promised he would be un-bossed, saying, "If you elect me, you will have elected a governor who has made no promises to any man." Taken literally, this was a dramatic reversal of the "ask the mayor" WPA job applicant policy of Governor Moore. One historian believes Hague dismissed Edison's words as mere "campaign rhetoric" by an amateur that would be quickly forgotten after the election. Edison won, with a 64,000-vote statewide plurality made possible by the 108,000 votes with which he carried Hudson County. Much to "Duh Mare's" chagrin, however, the new governor meant what he said, and the removal of Moore's private phone line to Jersey City's city hall was one of his first acts. That symbolic shot was the first fired in a series of skirmishes between Edison and the Hudson County boss in a struggle that, unsupported by his mentor in Washington, the governor mostly lost. Edison, considered somewhat haughty, perhaps because he was extremely hard of hearing, was a disaster as a politician—one of his supporters even conceded that he was "wholly unsuited for public life." In the process of his battle with Hague, however, the governor did succeed somewhat in advancing the case for constitutional reform, which eventually caused Hague's exit from public life.[131]

Although Frank Hague was no longer welcome at the scene of his greatest triumphs, Charles Edison and his wife moved to Sea Girt on July 7, 1941, for the now traditional gubernatorial summer residency. With the National Guard in federal service, the camp was quieter than usual, although soldiers from other states, like the officers of the 104th Observation Squadron of the Maryland National Guard, came to town for brief training courses. It was far from lonely at the Little White House, however, as the governor, his wife and two other family members (the Edisons were childless) were attended by eleven servants and a security guard of four state troopers and entertained a constant stream of visitors. The press eagerly anticipated the couple's participation in the "shore social season," including the "traditional official luncheon to members of the New Jersey Court of Pardons." The governor later stated that he only averaged five formal guests a day, not counting partygoers and casual drop-ins, and claimed that the Sea Girt house was simply a summertime government "workshop." Most of the work appears to have been political, however, as the Little White House became anti-Hague central headquarters in Edison's expanding intraparty squabble with the boss.[132]

The men of the New Jersey National Guard not only missed the Sea Girt summer of 1941, but the following four summers as well. In the aftermath of the December 7 Japanese attack on Pearl Harbor, the Guardsmen were informed that they were in service for the duration of the war. The installation saw some use by part-time State Guardsmen raised to replace the National Guard, but Sea Girt was soon swarming with soldiers again as the Army Signal Corps leased the camp property from the state for $125 a day, including electricity, water and gas, as a location to conduct basic training for recruits. Sea Girt—with mess hall space for 1,700 men, a post exchange and other buildings as well as its outstanding rifle range—provided a ready-made training site, even though it did not have much land on which to practice large-scale infantry maneuvers. Retaining the old New Jersey tradition of naming the camp after the governor in office, the Signal Corps dubbed the installation Camp Edison.[133]

The army crammed a lot of Signal Corps trainees into Camp Edison. Samuel Kaye of Bayonne, who eventually found himself in charge of sixteen-millimeter projector repairs in the European Theater of Operations, went through basic training at Sea Girt in 1943

Above: New Jersey Rifle Association headquarters, circa 1939. *Courtesy NGMMNJ.*

Right: Signal Corps trainees on Sea Girt beach, 1944. *Courtesy NGMMNJ.*

and recalled that the base was a sea of tents. The recruits drilled on the parade ground, fired on the ranges and conducted route marches up and down nearby highways and out into what is now Allaire State Park, where they performed tactical maneuvers. Kaye, a city boy who had never been "down the shore," didn't get a chance to participate in the local tourist scene. On his only weekend pass during the eight-week training period, he went home to Bayonne. There was some on-base social life for trainees, however, with local girls invited to occasional USO-sponsored dances. Nat Brooks and Terry Hughes, Manasquan High School students at the time, boarded a bus in Manasquan, got off a mile up the road in Sea Girt and transferred to a "rickety army bus that was waiting for the volunteer corps [of girls]." The dances were held in a large hall, where "a GI band belted out all the popular songs" as soldiers and Jersey girls "jitterbugged like crazy until the witching hour of ten o'clock."[134]

While the GIs jitterbugged, the governor mulled over an unpleasant reminder of his Sea Girt summer. Along with his problems with Frank Hague, Edison's year began with a controversy about his expenses. On February 19, 1942, the governor exploded about the $5,533.76 Little White House August food bill, which he had been stewing over since September 8. Edison wrote Brigadier General Stephen H. Barlow, the state's quartermaster general, complaining that the cost was "preposterous," and suggesting "some sort of swindle has been perpetrated," for which he held Barlow responsible. The accusations resulted in a nine-day state senate investigation producing nine hundred pages of testimony. In the past, most Little White House summer supplies had been ordered through the Camp Commissary at wholesale prices, but in 1941, with the National Guard in federal service, they were purchased at retail rates, mostly from Augustus Giunco's Sea Girt market. Giunco not only sold food directly, but also acted as a purchasing agent for items he did not normally stock, such as liquor, lobsters and baked goods for the governor's household. In addition to foodstuffs, in June the governor's staff had ordered $895.75 in unidentified goods from Maude T. Borab's shop in Spring Lake. The Borab store was a high-end "Trousseau Shop" featuring, among many other items, imported fine linen tablecloths with matching dinner napkins, and it is likely that Edison's household bought some of these for state luncheons and dinners.[135]

The investigation revealed a number of things, including that Edison's personal butler, George B. Milligan, had stocked up on "caviar, pate de foie gras, and truffles, all sorts of fancy imported delicacies," without regard to cost. Mrs. Edison served only white meat when chicken or turkey was on the menu. One senator asked Milligan "if five turkeys…would ordinarily suffice, how many turkeys would be necessary to serve the same quantity of meat if only white meat were used?" The butler responded that "it would take more than double—probably about twelve turkeys." In 1941, when poultry was priced comparatively with beef, this practice was viewed as far more profligate than today. In August 1941, for example, roasting chickens were thirty-six cents a pound, whole turkeys cost thirty-eight cents a pound and sirloin steak was forty cents a pound. Other disclosures revealed orders for large numbers of cigarettes, the existence of a perpetually open and unregulated bar and the fact that one staff member consumed numerous bottles of liquor and tossed the empties out a window at the governor's summer "workshop." In an embarrassing aside, Mr. Giunco testified that he was instructed to deceptively label Little White House liquor purchases as food on invoices. In the end, the all-Republican senate committee found the affair a "tempest in a teapot," as the expenses were covered by prior state appropriations for the governor's summer subsistence, although the senators did point out that sloppy record keeping should be corrected.[136]

The whole incident proved awkward, and Hague adherents used it to characterize the Edison-Hague fight as that of an elitist versus a man of the people. Filled with faux outrage, Hagueite Hudson County Assemblyman Peter Artaserse called for closing the Little White House "in the interests of public economy and to prevent scandal and the improper and extravagant use of public funds." Artaserse introduced a bill to "discontinue, once and for all, the Sea Girt Night club that is supported and maintained by the state." Adjutant General James I. Bowers prepared, but did not release, an angry response claiming "the Hague-Artaserse statement is so ridiculous that at first glace I was not inclined to even answer it. The statement was prepared by Hague and his stooges, and then handed to his puppet, Artaserse, for public gossip." In the middle of the tempest, Quartermaster General Barlow announced that he had ordered all of A. Harry Moore's Sea Girt bills burned, which did little to tone down the invective.[137]

Little White House dining room, circa 1935. *Courtesy NGMMNJ.*

The senate committee recommended that "under present war conditions, the use of the Sea Girt Cottage be dispensed with, unless it can be used in relation to some useful purpose connected with the prosecution of the war," and that recommendation was accepted. Although the 1942 "summer season" would not include Governor Edison's "Night club" by the sea, life went on in Sea Girt. Despite blackouts, dimouts and submarine scares, and the absence of the governor for the first time in the memory of many local folks, resort life, albeit much curtailed, endured. Private craft were missing from the ocean and inlets due to fuel rationing, but party fishing boats still plied the water close to shore and there was a revival of surf fishing. In June, the New Jersey Press Association held a three-day convention at the Stockton Hotel, and the hotel prepared for its annual Red, White and Blue Ball, which formally kicked off the summer social season. Although the National Guard was gone, there was still a decidedly "military flavor" to Sea Girt society, due to the Signal Corps officers stationed at Camp Edison.[138]

By June of 1942, the USO came up with a "useful purpose connected with the prosecution of the war" for the Little White House, requesting state permission to use the building as its Camp Edison headquarters. Adjutant General Bowers, however, was reluctant to let the governor's house be used for any purpose, citing the fact that the New Jersey Rifle Association building was already in use as an officers' club and that an enlisted men's recreation center was under construction at the camp. Bowers contended that, among other problems, the Little White House lacked a heating plant for winter use, and since it did not have a cellar, furnace installation would require excavation. He claimed that the cost of converting the house for USO use and subsequent postwar reconversion to fit it for state purposes again would be excessive. Despite his arguments, considerable pressure was brought to bear on Bowers, and the USO offered to spend $20,000 to upgrade the premises. Edison, perhaps still simmering over the ongoing food fight, finally stated that the military could use the "cottage" as it was, if they wished, but that the state would not make any modifications whatsoever.[139]

The New Jersey National Guard's 113th Infantry Regiment, based in Essex, Bergen, Hudson and Passaic Counties, was mobilized with the rest of the 44th Division in September 1940, and was stationed at Fort Dix. In the fall of 1941, the regiment, while in North Carolina on maneuvers, was detached from the 44th and assigned to the First Army. With the outbreak of war, the 113th was assigned to a "Combat Team" charged with the defense of a three-hundred-mile stretch of coastline from Long Island to Delaware, a mission it performed for the next twenty-seven months. It was in this role that New Jersey National Guard soldiers trained at Sea Girt ended up once more on New Jersey's beaches, serving as a combat-ready backup force for the Coast Guard.[140]

With the outbreak of war, the Coast Guard, which had absorbed the Lighthouse Service in 1939, extinguished the Sea Girt Lighthouse and removed its powerful Fresnel lens from the building. For the duration of the conflict, the keeper's quarters housed a sixteen-man Coast Guard garrison. "Coasties" were assigned to walk the beaches looking for ships in distress or enemy activity. Initial patrols by unarmed Coast Guardsmen carrying no weapons were "not taken seriously," until the arrest of eight Nazi saboteurs landed by a German submarine on Long Island in June 1942. The patrols quickly became more serious and heavily armed, and an army detachment moved in to camp on the Sea Girt Lighthouse lawn. Lighthouses like Sea Girt's provided ready-made lookouts, and were supplemented by observation towers erected along the beaches, all manned twenty-four hours a day. Coast Guard patrols usually consisted of two men armed with rifles, handguns and flare pistols. By August 1942 dogs were introduced to assist patrols in New Jersey, and mounted Coast Guardsmen astride former army cavalry horses were added in September.[141]

No Nazi saboteurs landed at Sea Girt, but as the summer of 1942 stretched on, the war drifted into the town's beaches. By late June, a seven-mile stretch of shore between Belmar and Manasquan, including Sea Girt, was covered with "oil and tar residue" and debris from sunken ships as the Nazis launched Operation Drumbeat, an all-out attack on American shipping, in which German submarines came so close to the coast that crewmen listened to local radio stations. Nat Brooks and Terry Hughes vividly remembered the chaos of that time over a half century later: "Fire whistles sounded often during the night. Local fishermen raced out to try to rescue seamen from the ocean on fire. Rumors flew [that] Germans had landed on the once pristine beach, now a goopy mess resulting from the torpedoed oilers." Allen Atheras, a youngster living in Spring Lake near Wreck Pond during the war, recalled that his mother left a bottle of turpentine alongside the back door to wipe beach tar off her children's bare feet. Along with wreckage and oil, empty life rafts were tossed ashore, and Atheras found a canvas

Sea Girt Lighthouse in 1938. *Courtesy Randy Gabrielan.*

holstered .45-caliber automatic pistol in one. In a bizarre counterpoint to the jumble of debris and petroleum waste littering the beachfront, summer guests at the great old hotels—the Monmouth and Essex and Sussex in Spring Lake and the Stockton in Sea Girt—strolled the boardwalk in evening dress as if there were no war. At the end of June, three hundred workers, sixty-five of them detailed from WPA projects, were deployed to clean the beaches so they could be used for bathing. The tide of war in American waters gradually turned as the navy instituted the convoy system and antisubmarine patrols took their toll, finishing the bloody "happy time" of the German submariners by the end of 1942.[142]

World War II intruded in other, very personal ways on Sea Girt, as permanent and summer residents entered the military. Richard S. Tucker, a nineteen-year-old lifeguard hero during the *Morro Castle* disaster and a three-sport athlete at Pingry and Hun Schools, was drafted in January 1941. Tucker, a native of Elizabeth who had been a Sea Girt lifeguard for six years in the 1930s, rose to the rank of sergeant before he was killed in action in North Africa on March 18, 1943. Sergeant Tucker was one of 17,172 New Jerseyans cut down in the prime of their lives by the war by the time it ended in 1945.[143]

After a shakedown period featuring economic dislocation, high unemployment levels and strikes in the immediate postwar period, the people of New Jersey left the long sad years of the Depression and World War II behind them. In the ensuing decade, the state entered an era of peace and prosperity, reflected in a flood of visitors to southern Monmouth County's beaches. Families began to rent cottages and bungalows for a

Stockton Hotel Beach, circa 1940. *Courtesy Randy Gabrielan.*

week or two in the summer again and day-tripping vacationers drove down the brand-new Garden State Parkway from densely populated northern New Jersey cities and burgeoning suburbs to enjoy the summertime surf and sand of the shore. By 1960, few tourists gave much if any thought to shark attacks. The last serious shark incident near Sea Girt had occurred over forty years before. On July 6, 1916, Essex and Sussex Hotel bellhop captain Charles Bruder had both of his legs sheared off below the knees by a shark while swimming off the hotel employees' beach in Spring Lake. Although Bruder, or what was left of him, was pulled into a lifeguard rescue boat, he bled to death before reaching shore, one of several fatalities attributed to sharks in Monmouth County that year.[144]

By 1960, however, Bruder's fate was long forgotten. There had been a shark scare in Spring Lake the previous summer, but that was no doubt far from the mind of John Brodeur when, on August 21, the twenty-four-year-old Jersey City accountant came to Sea Girt to visit his fiancée Jean Filoramo, a Jersey City teacher working as a summer waitress at the Stockton Hotel. Brodeur and Filoramo walked down to the Stockton's employee beach and the young man swam to bodysurf a wave in. Hit suddenly by a force he later said felt like a "Mack truck" pulling on his right leg, Brodeur saw the water go red around him. His fiancée and several onlookers pulled him to shore and he was rushed by ambulance to Fitkin Memorial Hospital in Neptune, where a surgeon worked four and a half hours to save his mangled limb. Despite the heroic efforts of the hospital staff, gangrene set in and Brodeur eventually lost the leg below the knee, but survived.[145]

Washington Boulevard looking east, circa 1955. *Courtesy Randy Gabrielan.*

For some, tragedy is opportunity. Following the Brodeur incident, several other swimmers were attacked by sharks along the New Jersey coast, and there were numerous "scares" without provenance. With shark news dominating local headlines, Monmouth County merchants, their normally lucrative Labor Day weekend in the offing, became increasingly nervous. As if by magic, however, two north Jersey entrepreneurs, Frank Arpin and Anthony Cataldo of Orange, appeared in Sea Girt within days of the Brodeur attack with a unique, if seemingly dubious at first glance, solution to the shark problem. On August 26, Arpin and Cataldo stretched a 75-foot-long "bubble fence" along the ocean floor 250 feet out from shore between the two jetties bordering the Stockton beach. Arpin proclaimed the "fence" to be a shark-proof barrier and claimed it had been thoroughly tested at an Asbury Park aquarium, where only one "wild, irritable, much handled shark" had penetrated it. Unfortunately, further testing of the device—consisting of a length of ventilated tubing through which compressed air was pumped to create upward flowing bubbles—failed not only to stop much handled sharks, but few at all. In a 1961 experiment conducted by the Office of Naval Research, ten of twelve tiger sharks passed through the bubble fence "undisturbed," or, as one report had it, "as if it were so much gossamer." It appears the inventors were either using the wrong type of shark for their tests or were counting on the relative rarity of New Jersey shark incidents to insulate them from being proved wrong.[146]

Memories of the bubble fence, along with worries of shark attacks, faded once more by 1962, replaced by an awe of nature's destructive power when a hurricane severely battered Sea Girt's shoreline. The storm broke up the boardwalk and washed much of the borough's beach out to sea. At least as disturbing to some, the following years witnessed the passing of two of Sea Girt's most enduring landmarks, the Stockton Hotel and the Little White House. Thoughts of a possible fire at the Stockton were a source of significant anxiety to Sea Girt's little volunteer fire department over the years. The fire company, with its two pumping engines, one ladder truck and forty-five members, had extinguished two blazes at the hotel with aid from nearby fire companies, but the old building, with some parts of its structure dating back to 1875, was a virtual tinderbox. The era of the big luxury hotels was rapidly waning along the Jersey Shore by the 1960s, due to the public's changing vacation habits. By the early 1960s, modernization was fiscally out of the question and maintenance deferred as the once-grand old hostelry slipped into genteel shabbiness. One visitor found himself in a tiny room illuminated by a bulb dangling from the ceiling on exposed wiring. The Stockton's owner closed it in 1962 and petitioned the borough to allow him to tear the building down and replace it with a modern structure. The proposal met with, at best, a mixed response from the people and borough government of Sea Girt. Following a number of hearings and at least one lawsuit, however, the plan was approved in the summer of 1965. On September 17 and 18 the hotel held a sale of its furniture, fixtures, china and anything else buyers could carry away, with demolition scheduled for the following week.[147]

The wrecking crew would not be needed. On the early evening of Thursday, September 23, fire broke out in the south section of the hotel. Although the Sea Girt Fire Company responded minutes later, the conflagration raced through the old building, aided by open windows that acted like flues. Jack Geiger, on his way home from work to Spring Lake, recalls seeing a plume of smoke from the burning hotel rise into the early evening sky as he drove down the Garden State Parkway, miles away to the north. Within an hour, despite the efforts of firemen from Sea Girt, Manasquan and Spring Lake, the Stockton was clearly doomed. The police denied any vehicles but fire trucks entry to town as companies from the surrounding area continued to respond and the task at hand changed from extinguishing the blaze to preventing its spread to neighboring homes. In the end, over sixty pieces of firefighting equipment were deployed by forty-three companies drawing water from Wreck Pond, Stockton Lake and even the ocean to contain the inferno. Exhausted firefighters continued the battle all night, supplied with food and drink by the women's auxiliaries of the Sea Girt, Manasquan and Spring Lake companies. By morning, the Stockton Hotel was gone forever. Peter Anderson has vivid memories of its going. Anderson, eight years old at the time, had a ringside seat on the second-floor porch of his friend's house a few blocks south of the hotel. When the fire hit the kitchen, generations of grease fueled a bizarre light show streaming skyward. "You could see orange, blue and red flames, and all shades in between," he recalled. "It was like the Fourth of July."[148]

The Little White House was next, but its going was more drawn out. New Jersey changed wartime governors in 1944 with the election of Republican Walter E. Edge, who returned to office for his second wartime term. Neither Edge, the last governor to serve under the 1844 Constitution, nor his successors—Alfred E. Driscoll, Robert B. Meyner, Richard J. Hughes or William Cahill, all elected to four-year terms under the new Constitution of 1947—chose to reopen the Little White House or spend the summer in Sea Girt. One state official recalled that Driscoll, an energetic and reform-minded governor, "scolded previous administrations for throwing lavish parties" at Sea Girt. Most of the house's furnishings were eventually dispersed to Morven, the Princeton home donated to the state as a governor's residence by Governor Edge (and ironically the ancestral home of the Stocktons), and a new gubernatorial summer home established at Island Beach State Park to the south. In 1955, Governor Meyner suggested making the mansion and its immediate surroundings a state park, but the plan failed to materialize. In 1966, a board of National Guard officers, chaired by Colonel Wilfred G. Menard Jr., was appointed to consider the fate of the abandoned Little White House.[149]

Menard's report suggested three possible outcomes for the historic house. In order of preference and desirability, they were: 1) Demolish the wing erected by Governor Larson in 1929 and restore the original building for use as a state military museum and/or transfer it to the state Historic Sites Commission; 2) Restore the main house for use as a museum and renovate the Larson addition to house the staff and faculty of the National Guard Officer Candidate School; 3) Demolish the entire structure.[150]

The report described the house as a frame structure of "modified Georgian design" set upon a stone foundation, with a cedar shingle roof and two wooden porches, one with a flagstone floor. The interior, including the newer west wing, with kitchen, pantry and staff bedrooms, contained forty plaster-walled rooms. A rotunda-style entrance foyer led to a reception room and curved stairway to the second floor. Although another report of the

Little White House as it looked after World War II. *Courtesy NGMMNJ.*

same era described the house as "badly deteriorated by time and the ravages of coastal weather," and a "sad reminder of happier days," this assessment was incorrect. Brigadier General (retired) Jeffrey Pierson, current director of the National Guard Training Center (NGTC), graduated from officers' candidate school at Sea Girt in 1964, and recalled attending classes in the mansion, which he described as being in "great shape" at that time. The officer panel of 1966 reported that although "the building has not been used for 25 years, the state of repair is relatively good." A 1968 account of the interior described a boarded-up fireplace, peeling paint and dust from falling ceiling plaster on the reception-room floor, but an essentially sound structure. This assessment is supported by General Pierson, who visited the building that year and recalled that the deterioration appeared readily repairable. The assessing officers considered the real estate value of the house; "with approximately 10,000 feet of floor space and at today's [1966] value the replacement cost of this building would be between 200 and 250 thousand dollars."[151]

Many Sea Girt residents wanted to preserve this monument to their town's role in state and national history. Mayor John G. Rodgers waxed nostalgic, noting that although "Governor Hughes seems to prefer Morven at Princeton, and that's his privilege…it would be nice to have governors come back." Conceding he found the mansion "a nice reminder of what it once was," Councilman Jack Richards said that "when you match nostalgia against cost, from the state's point of view, you have to be practical." Longtime Sea Girt resident Mrs. Munroe Hawes, whose garden club sponsored a flower show in the building in 1963, was reluctant to see it torn down, although she admitted there was not enough heat in the house for winter use and that the plumbing was in need of renovation. Despite the dire possibilities, however, it initially appeared that the report might have saved the Little White House. A newspaper article published the following April noted that "the building is now being converted to house a museum…principally of state history and past wars." In June 1967, State Treasurer John A. Kervick, acting on behalf of Governor Hughes, notified Adjutant General James F. Cantwell that the recommendation to "demolish the wing and restore the original building for use as a military museum is approved," and that $75,000 had been set aside in the forthcoming fiscal year budget for the project. As late as April 1969, when it was announced that the State Police Academy would be moving to Sea Girt, the public was advised that the Little White House had a future as a museum.[152]

Something went awry. Despite the promises, nothing was done to implement the board's recommendation, the funds were not expended and the issue was ignored for several more years. In 1971, officials in Governor William T. Cahill's administration ordered the house razed to save the $8,000 a year allocated to maintain it. Although the garden clubs of New Jersey expressed interest in using the building as a headquarters, and the Sea Girt Women's Club petitioned the state to save it, there was, unfortunately, no substantial public or political outcry against its destruction. The Little White House's last official occupant, Charles Edison, for whom it had proved a political liability, passed away on July 31, 1969. A journalist from the *Newark Sunday News* (soon to be history itself) concluded that the memories and ghosts of the Saint Louis Exposition, Woodrow Wilson, Franklin D. Roosevelt and other luminaries who trod the steps of the old governor's summer home were insufficient reasons to rescue it. It was, this Philistine thought, "simply a big old house like any other big old house." He concluded that those for whom the house had meaning were as long gone as its occupants and that "in the age of progress and questionable government spending it seems to fall in line that the money to keep up this deteriorating relic would do better in a needier coffer." Likely that money never got to a needier coffer, and a significant piece of Sea Girt, New Jersey and United States history was tragically consigned to oblivion when bids for its destruction were solicited on March 9, 1971.[153]

There would be one last dance. On April 3, 1971, the Little White House "once again heard the sounds of conversation, laughter, music and tinkling glasses, and saw guests enjoying its charm and beauty" as the scene of the annual dinner dance of the Carnation Ball Committee of Sea Girt's Saint Mark's Roman Catholic Church. Ninety people attended the celebration, as Sea Girt bade final farewell to a significant reminder of its rich past. Governor Cahill was invited, but failed to make an appearance, securing Charles Edison's place as the last governor to spend any real time there. The St. Mark's Committee held its Carnation Ball that summer, as in summers past, under a striped marquee on the Little White House lawn, but it is doubtful the ghosts of FDR, A. Harry Moore and Frank Hague lingered to witness it.[154]

With the Stockton and Little White House things of the past, few significant nineteenth-century Sea Girt landmarks remained, and they were endangered. The old Tremont Hotel went through a succession of owners and uses and then, with its top floors sliced off, became the Yankee Clipper, a popular seasonal watering hole, but was eventually razed to produce building lots. Although endangered by "progress," some very significant historic buildings were saved, however. The Coast Guard decommissioned the Sea Girt Lighthouse in 1945 and replaced its Fresnel lens with an automatic blinking light set atop the tower. That light, in turn, was moved in 1954 to a steel tower erected on the lighthouse north lawn, which was, in its turn, removed in 1977. The borough of Sea Girt bought the lighthouse in 1956 for $11,000 and subsequently used the building as a library, recreation and community center. By 1980, however, the borough considered razing the deteriorating structure and selling its exceptionally valuable beachfront property. A committee of local citizens went door to door raising funds and invested a good deal of sweat equity as well and succeeded in saving the lighthouse, eventually restoring it to its historic grandeur. Another relic of Sea Girt's early days, the Parker House Hotel, still stands a block away from the restored lighthouse, and is a well-regarded bar and restaurant offering summer lodging. The train doesn't stop at Sea Girt anymore, but the old New York and Long Branch Railroad station, where thousands of National Guardsmen on their way to camp and Democrats coming to hail their candidates stepped off a train, is now the borough library. The old tenant farmer's home that served as the original Little White House outlived its successor and still stands within the boundaries of the National Guard Training Center.[155]

On the occasion of the June 1975 centennial celebrations of the Sea Girt Land Improvement Company's initial lot offering, an *Asbury Park Press* reporter wrote a feature article on the borough. The title, "Sea Girt Has Changed Little during 100-Year History," seemed contradicted by its illustrations, which included the Little White House, the Stockton Hotel, the Country Club racetrack and Camp Cedar, none still standing. The only surviving building pictured was the lighthouse, itself only a few years away from barely escaping oblivion. The article was generally factually correct, save for the assertion that the Little White House was where "Franklin D. Roosevelt learned of his nomination as the Democratic candidate for president," no doubt a conflation of the Wilson notification and the Roosevelt rally into each other—Frank Hague was already forgotten. Mayor Thomas Black, one of the heroic lifeguards of the *Morro Castle* disaster, told the reporter that Sea Girt, which in the years since World War II had become more a residential community than a resort, had "very little undeveloped land left and none of that is zoned for industry. We wanted a family town and that is what has developed." Frank Durand, once "residential director" of the old Sea Girt Company and honorary grand marshal of the centennial parade, noted that "when I first settled here in 1919, this was a nice residential area—although it was sparsely settled then." Durand's further assertion that "Sea Girt has changed very little since then" could be challenged, but his conclusion that "it was one of the nicest areas on the shore then, and it still is," could not.

Mr. Durand's statement to the contrary, Sea Girt changed a great deal in the decades following World War II, and continued to do so after 1975. The town was no longer

Sea Girt town library. *Courtesy of the author.*

Interior of the Sea Girt Inn, a well-known watering place for college students and summer revelers in the 1960s and 1970s. Actually in Wall Township, it was torn down in the 1990s. *Courtesy Randy Gabrielan.*

the epicenter of New Jersey political and military life it had been in the first half of the twentieth century. Governor Edison's 1942 food bill fight was the last New Jersey political drama to play out against a Sea Girt backdrop, and although the sitting governor still sponsors and attends an annual Governor's Day review at the National Guard Training Center, the summer capital is no more. By the 1950s, the National Guard camp was no longer swarming with troops throughout the summer. Military training had become more complex, and the New Jersey National Guard was no longer a light infantry division supplemented by some cavalrymen and a few observation aircraft that could take off across the beach from the drill field. The post–World War II Guard was a modern force with large numbers of vehicles, tanks and artillery, which conducted most of its training elsewhere, usually at Camp (now Fort) Drum in upstate New York. Actually, the New Jersey National Guard artillery, in need of long practice ranges, had been training at that location, then Pine Camp, since 1928. When Point Pleasant native Fred Burns joined the National Guard at Sea Girt in June 1948, there was only one unit holding drills there, the 141st Transportation Company. The regular army closed Fort Dix in 1992, but that base was reopened by the Army Reserve Command in 1997. Much Guard training at present is conducted there.

The Sea Girt center is still home to the National Guard Militia Museum of New Jersey and the 254th Regiment, a training unit that supervises the National Guard's Officer Candidate School. Other National Guard units headquartered at Sea Girt include the 63rd Army Band, Detachment 1, C Company; 250th Brigade Support Battalion (BSB); the New Jersey State Medical Detachment of Joint Forces Headquarters; the 154th Quartermaster Company; and the New Jersey National Guard Recruit Holding Company, as well as the New Jersey State Police and Department of Justice Academies. Some National Guard units still deploy to active duty out of Sea Girt, including C Troop of the 117th Cavalry and B Company, 250th BSB, in the summer of 2005. Community organizations use on-base athletic fields and a croquet green and there is an annual Irish Festival on the state property, which also hosts occasional Boy Scout jamborees. The training center beach is accessible by permit to active and retired members of the National Guard and their families.[156]

In the last decades of the twentieth century, Sea Girt more than fulfilled Frank Durand's other assessment as a "nice residential area." While many people continued to maintain or rent Sea Girt homes as summer residences, the borough's progress toward a year-round community is graphically illustrated in census figures that reveal 599 permanent residents in 1940 and 1,178 in 1950. By 1970, the permanent population had stabilized, and 2,148 people lived in the town at the time of the 2000 census, at which date 302 of the 1,285 housing units in the borough were available for seasonal rental. The first aerial photograph of Sea Girt, taken from a military aircraft in 1926, provides a perspective looking north from the National Guard Camp into a largely vacant southern section of town. A 1935 aerial photo from a different angle shows a similar lack of development in the lots immediately adjoining the camp. A 1948 aerial image, however, graphically reveals a significant increase in construction in Sea Girt proper, with the empty lots of previous years now filled with houses, although much

Wall Township land to the west was still farmland. Today, Sea Girt's Wall Township hinterland is fully developed as well.[157]

As the borough's population quadrupled, real estate prices rose significantly, and recent years have seen the loss of some of the once ubiquitous, sometimes stucco-faced classic "Sea Girter" houses, "with columns and porches and sloped roofs," that were purchased and torn down by builders in search of more square footage of living space. In 2002, at the height of the last real estate boom, a travel writer characterized Sea Girt's "one square mile of first-class real estate" as "well manicured and inviting," adding, with considerable insight, that "if it is possible for a shore town with an average home price in the neighborhood of $800,000 to be cozy and unpretentious, it is." The exciting days of political, military and shipwreck headlines featuring Sea Girt are long gone, but no one seems to miss them much, and the quiet little town seems a perfect fit with its current winter and summer residents.[158]

Ironically, considering its iconic status as a resort and political and military venue prior to 1941, Sea Girt has been largely ignored in New Jersey travel books published in the years following World War II. While the 1939 WPA guide to the state proclaimed the borough's status as "New Jersey's summer capital," National Guard training site and former summer home of the formidable Robert Stockton, by 1965 an "Official State

Aerial view of Sea Girt, looking north, 1948. *Courtesy New Jersey State Archives.*

"Sea Girter" house. *Courtesy of the author.*

Sea Girt beachfront, from north, 2008. *Courtesy of the author.*

Guide" bypassed the town entirely in a discussion of Monmouth County shore resorts, as did guidebooks from 1998 and 2001.[159]

Sea Girt has not forgotten its history, however. Nor will it. The lighthouse, saved by concerned citizens, has become a museum reflecting not only its own history, but that of Sea Girt as well. Housing period furniture, photos, maps, artifacts and artwork, including the possessions of some of its keepers, the museum presents the story of the lighthouse itself, and Sea Girt's past, notably, but not limited to, the *Morro Castle* disaster. The New Jersey National Guard Militia Museum, on the grounds of the National Guard Training Center and open to the public, tells the tale of New Jersey's military from colonial times to the present, and has a standing exhibit detailing the relationship between the National Guard and Sea Girt. Included in the exhibit are some souvenirs of the destroyed governor's mansion, including outside porch and interior stairway balusters, as well as the state crest shield that hung above the Little White House front door when the governor was in residence. A park across from the old train station is the site of a more recent monument honoring three Sea Girt men—Edward A. "Ted" Brennan III, Charles W. Mathers and Bill Mathesen—who lost their lives in the World Trade Center terrorist attack of September 11, 2001, as well as a memorial to Sea Girt residents who served in the nation's wars. As these words were written, rumors flew that the state of New Jersey, in one of its periodic budget crunches, was considering selling or leasing the historic land the NGTC stands on. The governor's office refused to confirm or deny such a plan, but local legislators came out strongly against any such disposition of the property.[160]

Sea Girt World Trade Center memorial. *Courtesy of the author.*

Sea Girt wars memorial. *Courtesy of the author.*

Original Little White House, 2008. *Courtesy of the author.*

They are all gone now, the Lenape, salt makers, Tory raiders, politicians, eccentrics, entrepreneurs and celebrities who trod the Sea Girt sand; Commodore Stockton, the Thurlow brothers, Elliston Morris, William J. Sewell, Leon Abbett, J. Madison Drake, Woodrow Wilson, Frank Hague, A. Harry Moore, Harold Hoffman, Charles Edison, Al Smith, Franklin D. Roosevelt and Frank Durand, along with the thousands of vacationers who danced the night away at the Beach House, the wagonloads of Guardsmen singing and yelling their way back from Manasquan and Neptune City, the farmers who bathed in their clothes in the August surf, the lighthouse keepers whose attention to duty saved ships at sea, the *Morro Castle* rescuers, the hordes of Jerseyans assembled by Frank Hague and the generations of part-time soldiers who sweated away summer days on the rifle range and then went off to war—some never to return. The square mile of history that is Sea Girt has seen them come and go for hundreds of years, and it keeps their secrets, but lightly. It takes a little prying to discover those stories today, but they are still there, floating as ether in the atmosphere, and if you listen quietly in the night, when the wind is right, and let your imagination run free, you can hear them still.

APPENDIX

Historical Sites and Museums in Sea Girt

National Guard Militia Museum of New Jersey

The National Guard Training Center in Sea Girt, located at Sea Girt Avenue and Camp Drive, is home to the National Guard Militia Museum of New Jersey. The museum is open to the public and presents the role of the New Jersey Militia and National Guard within the context of the larger history of the state, using original and reproduction uniforms, weapons, photographs, artifacts and art from the period of Dutch, Swedish and British colonization through the War for Independence, Civil War and World Wars I and II to the present day, paying particular attention to the diversity of the New Jersey citizen soldier and his or her experience, as well as presenting a standing exhibit on the relationship between Sea Girt and the National Guard. The museum supports annexes in Lawrenceville and in the Trenton War Memorial.

The museum is also home to the Center for U.S. War Veterans' Oral History Project, an official partner of the Library of Congress Veterans' History Project. It is the center's mission to collect and preserve the memories of veterans through recorded oral history interviews. The interviews are recorded on videotape and DVD formats and housed at the Library of Congress and the museum's Sea Girt location, where they are accessible to researchers and scholars. To date, the center's collection contains over three hundred interviews of veterans of all branches of service from World War II, Korea, Vietnam, Desert Storm, Operation Iraqi Freedom and other American military campaigns.

The museum is open Tuesdays, Wednesdays and Thursdays and on selected weekends throughout the year from 10:00 a.m. to 3:00 p.m. Group tours are welcome with prior notice. For further information on visitation, group tours, research or to participate in the oral history program, call 732.974.5966 or visit the website at http://www.nj.gov/military/museum/index.html.

The Sea Girt Lighthouse

The Sea Girt Lighthouse, saved from being razed by concerned citizens who incorporated as the Sea Girt Lighthouse Citizens' Committee in 1981, leases the lighthouse from the

National Guard Militia Museum of New Jersey (NGMMNJ), 2008. *Courtesy of the author.*

NGMMNJ's New Jersey in the Civil War exhibit. *Courtesy of the author.*

The Sea Girt Lighthouse, 2008. *Courtesy of the author.*

Lighthouse *Morro Castle* exhibit. *Courtesy of the author.*

borough of Sea Girt. In the years since, the committee has restored the lighthouse itself and added period furniture, historic photos, maps and other artifacts to present the historic structure's story to the public. Included among the displays are a replica of the weight that turned the rotating tower lens, an authentic fourth-order Fresnel lens similar to the original one and artifacts from the *Morro Castle* disaster that washed up on Sea Girt's beach that fateful September of 1934.

The lighthouse is open to the public on Sundays between 2:00 and 4:00 p.m. from April through November. Tours are available for school, Scout and other groups. The Lighthouse Citizens' Committee also sponsors events, including an art show and the annual fall New Jersey Lighthouse Challenge that bring many people to the lighthouse, which has become an integral part of the community and a widely recognized symbol of Sea Girt. For more information, contact the Sea Girt Lighthouse Citizens' committee, Inc., PO Box 83, Sea Girt, NJ, 08750 (732.974.0514), or visit the website, http://www.lonekeep.com/seagirtlighthouse/.

Notes

Chapter 1

1. Paul D. Boyd, *Atlantic Highlands: From Lenape Camps to Bayshore Town* (Charleston, SC: Arcadia, 2004), 12–13; Abstract of New Jersey Army National Guard Phase I Archeological Surveys: Sea Girt and Morristown (Trenton, n.d.); Alanson Skinner and Max Schrabisch, comps., *A Preliminary Report of the Archeological Survey of the State of New Jersey* (Trenton: McCrellish & Quigley, 1913), 48; Peter Anderson interview, February 15, 2008.

2. Clyde L. MacKenzie Jr., *The Fisheries of Raritan Bay* (New Brunswick: Rutgers University Press, 1992), 14–15; Boyd, *Atlantic Highlands*, 14–15.

3. Gregory Evans Dowd, *The Indians of New Jersey* (Trenton: New Jersey Historical Commission, 1992), 31–32; Boyd, *Atlantic Highlands*, 25–26; George H. Moss Jr., *Monmouth—Our Indian Heritage* (Freehold, NJ: Monmouth County Historical Commission, 4th ed., 2000), 32.

4. Moss, *Monmouth*, 32.

5. Ibid., 34–35.

6. Hubert G. Schmidt, *Agriculture in New Jersey: A Three Hundred Year History* (New Brunswick: Rutgers University Press, 1973), 25.

7. Boyd, *Atlantic Highlands*, 30; Schmidt, *Agriculture in New Jersey*, 26–27.

8. John E. Pomfret, *The Province of East New Jersey, 1609–1702* (Princeton: Princeton University Press, 1962), 42.

9. Edwin Salter, *A History of Monmouth and Ocean Counties* (Bayonne, NJ: Gardner & Sons, 1890), 33–34; Dowd, *Indians of New Jersey*, 47, 58–59; Harold F. Wilson, *The Story of the New Jersey Shore* (Princeton: D. Van Nostrand Company, 1964), 3; Boyd, *Atlantic Highlands*, 24.

10. Miriam V. Studley, ed. *Historic New Jersey Through Visitors' Eyes* (Princeton: D. Van Nostrand, 1964), 7. For details of Dutch attempts to colonize Monmouth County, see Boyd, *Atlantic Highlands*, 30–33.

11. Peter O. Wacker, *Land and People: A Cultural Geography of Preindustrial New Jersey: Origins and Settlement Patterns* (New Brunswick: Rutgers University Press, 1975), 58; Dowd, *Indians of New Jersey*, 50–51; Moss, *Monmouth*, 33; Salter, *Monmouth and Ocean Counties*, 116–17; Herbert C. Kraft and John T. Kraft, *The Indians of Lenapehoking* (Elizabeth, NJ: Lenape Books, 1985), 39.

12. Anthony F.C. Wallace, *King of the Delawares: Teedyuscung*, 1700–1763 (Philadelphia: University of Pennsylvania Press, 1949), 2; George L. Tootell, "The History of Crescent Park," unpublished monograph in the NGMMNJ collection; Salter, *History of Monmouth and Ocean Counties*, 306; Kraft and Kraft, *Indians of Lenapehoking*, 39. Discoveries at Burlington County's Burr-Haines archaeological site provide a rare look at mid-eighteenth-century New Jersey Native American life. Cuff links and pins found indicate that residents wore European-style clothing. Other evidence suggests a lifestyle making use of ancient technologies, including stone tool making, along with European goods, including metal knives and spoons and lead shot. Animal bones indicated a diet of wild game, supplemented by pigs, but not sheep, cattle or chickens. Richard Veit, *Digging New Jersey's Past: Historical Archeology in the Garden State* (New Brunswick: Rutgers University Press, 2002), 58–62.

13. Wilson, *Jersey Shore*, 7–8; Moss, *Monmouth*, 31–33; Maxine N. Lurie and Marc Mappen, eds., *Encyclopedia of New Jersey* (New Brunswick, Rutgers University Press, 2004), 20–22.

14. For an account of political battles and personalities in seventeenth-century East Jersey, see Pomfret, *Province of East Jersey*.
15. Schmidt, *Agriculture in New Jersey*, 8; Wacker, *Land and People*, 12–13; Wilson, *Jersey Shore*, 8–9; Wacker, *Land and People*, 128.
16. A.M. Thomas Thompson, *Two Missionary Voyages, 1745–1756* (London: Society for Promoting Christian Knowledge facsimile reprint, 1937), 18–19.
17. For a synopsis of the internal struggle in Monmouth County, see Katherine A. Bilby, "'The Enemy Amongst Us': The Revolution as Civil War in Monmouth County, New Jersey, 1776–1783" (master's thesis, Brooklyn College).
18. Harry B. Weiss and Grace M. Weiss, *The Revolutionary Saltworks of the New Jersey Coast* (Trenton: Past Times Press, 1959), 12; Salter, *Monmouth and Ocean Counties*, 274.
19. Weiss and Weiss, *Revolutionary Saltworks*, 13.
20. Ibid., 14–16; John W. Barber and Henry Howe, *Historical Collections of the State of New Jersey...* (New Haven, CT: Benjamin Olds, 1844), 351.
21. Weiss and Weiss, *Revolutionary Saltworks*, 18–20.
22. Wilson, *Jersey Shore*, 19–20.
23. Lurie and Mappen, eds., *Encyclopedia of New Jersey*, 392, 596, 844.
24. Thomas F. Gordon, *The History of New Jersey from its Discovery by Europeans to the Adoption of the Federal Constitution* (Trenton: Daniel Fenton, 1834), 242; Barber and Howe, *Historical Collections*, 350.

Chapter 2
25. Wheaton J. Lane, *From Indian Trail to Iron Horse: Travel and Transportation in New Jersey, 1620–1860* (Princeton: Princeton University Press, 1939), 332; *New York Times*, October 9, 1866.
26. *The National Cyclopedia of American Biography*, vol. 2 (New York: James T. White & Co., 1895), 7.
27. Ibid., 332, 334–35. An excellent summary of the Joint Companies' political maneuvering is provided in Thomas Fleming, *New Jersey: A History* (New York: W.W. Norton, 1977), 101–07. Fee manipulation is covered in Roger Avery Barton, "The Camden and Amboy Railroad Monopoly," *Proceedings of the New Jersey Historical Society* 12, no. 4 (October 1927). For a detailed study of the Joint Companies' activities, see George Reilly, "The Camden and Amboy Railroad in New Jersey Politics" (PhD dissertation, Columbia University).
28. Ann Blackman, "Fatal Cruise of the Princeton," *Navy History* (September 2005).
29. K. Jack Bauer, *The Mexican War, 1846–1848* (New York: MacMillan, 1974), 172–96, 369.
30. *New York Times*, January 28, 1852.
31. Richard O. Venino, *History of Sea Girt: Fiftieth Anniversary, 1917–1967* (privately printed, 1967), 4–5.
32. *New York Times*, June 26, 1892; Franklin Ellis, *History of Monmouth County, New Jersey* (Philadelphia: R.T. Peck & Co.), 804; "Sea Girt's First Military Ball Held Thirty Years Ago in Stockton Home," unidentified, undated (1915) newspaper clipping in NGMMNJ collection; John T. Cunningham, *The New Jersey Shore* (New Brunswick: Rutgers University Press, 1958), 64.
33. "Sea Girt's First Military Ball"; Gustave Kobbe, *The Jersey Coast and Pines* (Short Hills, NJ; 1889), 56; Lewis Historical Publishing Company, *History of Monmouth County New Jersey 1664–1920*, vol. 2 (Chicago and New York: Lewis, 1922), 520–21; Tootell, "History of Crescent Park"; *New York Times*, January 28, 1852.
34. *New York Times*, July 24, 1856; Lewis Historical Publishing, *Monmouth County*, 521.
35. *New York Times*, January 26, 1860; Fleming, *New Jersey*, 118; Ellis, *History of Monmouth County*, 804.
36. *New York Times*, June 20, 1863; October 9, 1866; Ellis, *History of Monmouth County*, 804; Deed Book 190, 385, Monmouth County Archives.
37. Tootell, "History of Crescent Park"; Wilson, *Jersey Shore*, 46; *New York Times*, July 21, 1873.
38. Morris Family Papers, MCHA, Folder #1; Venino, *History of Sea Girt*, iii, 14. Deed Book 207, 288; Deed Book 229, 386; Deed Book 268, 423, Monmouth County Archives. An 1899 memo from the Sea Girt Land Improvement Company in the Morris family papers, Folder #1, indicates the company was initially chartered in 1869. There seems a tendency for early Philadelphia/Sea Girt families to sell

property to each other. A survey of property exchanges in the James Hunter family by Monmouth County Archives Research Assistant Mary Ann Kiernan revealed that in 1878 Hunter, an Irish-born Philadelphia clock manufacturer and president of the Land Improvement Company, purchased lots from his own company and that they were traded back and forth among his children and other relations throughout the 1880s and 1890s.
39. Morris Family Papers, MCHA, Folder #1; Tootell, "History of Crescent Park"; Venino, *Sea Girt*, 16; Deed Book 306, 461, Monmouth County Archives; Lewis Historical Publishing, *Monmouth County*, 525.
40. Morris Family Papers.
41. *Hopewell Herald*, September 21, 1881; Kobbe, *Jersey Coast and Pines*, 56; Wilson, *Jersey Shore*, 46; Cunningham, *New Jersey Shore*, 65; "Sea Girt's First Military Ball"; Don Wood, Joel Rosenbaum and Tom Gallo, *The Unique New York and Long Branch* (Earlton, NY: Audio-Visual Designs, 1985), 20, 48–49.
42. Boyd, *Atlantic Highlands*, 12; Charles D. Wrege, *Spring Lake: An Early History* (Spring Lake: Bicentennial History Committee, 1976), 45; Lewis Historical Publishing, *Monmouth County*, 478; WPA Federal Writers' Project, *New Jersey: A Guide to its Present and Past* (New York: Viking Press, 1939), 132, 592; Margaret Thomas Buchholz, ed., *Shore Chronicles: Diaries and Traveler's Tales from the Jersey Shore, 1764–1955* (Harvey Cedars, NJ: Down the Shore Publishing, 1999), 166–67.
43. Henry Charlton Beck, *The Roads of Home: Lanes and Legends of New Jersey* (New Brunswick: Rutgers University Press, 1956), 226.
44. Wrege, *Spring Lake*, 45; *New York Times*, August 21, 1885; August 13, 1893; Beck, *Roads of Home*, 228–29.
45. *New York Times*, August 11, 1895; Wilson, *Jersey Shore*, 9.
46. *Trenton Times*, August 10, 1901.
47. Beck, *Roads of Home*, 228. Most references to the farmers' summer surf party refer to it as Salt Water Day, but it also has been commonly called Big Sea Day since the 1950s. The first reference to the celebration as "Big Sea Day" dates from 1885. *New York Times*, August 21, 1885.
48. *New York Times*, August 21, 1885.

Chapter 3

49. Annual Report of the Adjutant General of the State of New Jersey for the Year 1869 (Trenton, 1870), 5–6. Hereafter cited as NJAG Report for 1884, 1885, etc. For the details of Civil War marksmanship training, or the lack thereof, see Joseph G. Bilby, *Small Arms at Gettysburg* (Yardley, PA: Westholme, 2007).
50. NJAG Report for 1883, 6, 39–40.
51. Manasquan Chamber of Commerce, *Manasquan* (Lewiston, ME: Geiger Brothers, 1962).
52. Ibid.
53. NJAG Report for 1884, 45, 47.
54. Sea Girt Camp, undated monograph in NGMMNJ collection.
55. "The Sea Girt Encampment," Morris Family papers, MCHA, Folder #1; *Camden Daily Courier*, April 23, 1891; "Sea Girt's First Military Ball"; Lewis, *History of Monmouth County*, 527.
56. Manasquan Chamber of Commerce, *Manasquan*; Map of Sea Girt Situated in Monmouth County, New Jersey, Charles F. Ingham, engineer, revised by Frederick J. Anspach, engineer, 1877, Monmouth County Archives, Freehold, NJ; Lewis, *History of Monmouth County*, 479–80; Floyd W. Parsons, ed., *New Jersey: Life, Industries and Resources of a Great State* (Newark: New Jersey State Chamber of Commerce, 1927), 47; *New York Times*, September 3, 1887; *Camden Daily Courier*, April 23, 1891.
57. NJAG Report for 1885, 79. A review of property transaction records for Sea Girt between 1885 and 1907 conducted by the author and Monmouth County Archives Research Assistant Mary Ann Kiernan on December 12, 2005, revealed one purchase by the State of New Jersey, a small addition to the Sea Girt Camp acquired in 1907 to add to the rifle range. This absence of records was confirmed by a telephone interview with Richard O. Venino, Esq., on December 13, 2005. Mr. Venino, author of a 1967 history of Sea Girt, stated that his own research had failed to uncover any records of title transfer of the current land occupied by the National Guard Training Center in the 1885–1907 period to the State of New Jersey save the 1907 document. Mr. Venino stated that he had, some "10 or 15 years ago," prepared a deed to formalize the de facto transfer, and presented it to state authorities.

For a detailed study of Leon Abbett's rise from hatter's son to governor of New Jersey, see Richard A. Hogarty, *Leon Abbett's New Jersey: The Emergence of the Modern Governor* (Philadelphia: American Philosophical Society, 2001).
58. All property transfer records cited were reviewed by the author with Monmouth County Archives Research Assistant Mary Ann Kiernan on January 7, 2008.
59. Kobbe, *Jersey Coast and Pines*, 56.
60. NJAG Report for 1886, 6, 23; *New York Times*, August 21, 1885; *Trenton Times*, August 21, 1885. Boat howitzers were small muzzleloading artillery pieces on cast-iron carriages. Two examples are on public display at the Asbury Park, New Jersey Civil War monument.
61. "Sea Girt's First Military Ball."
62. NJAG Report for 1888, 38–41, 44; NJAG Report for 1889, 52–53; NJAG Report for 1884, 50; NJAG Report for 1891, 36.
63. J. Madison Drake, *Historical Sketches of the Revolutionary and Civil Wars* (New York: Webster Press, 1908), 198, 262–67.
64. Ibid. The other Medal of Honor winners included Rufus King and Julian Scott.
65. *New York Times*, November 29, 1913; NJAG Report for 1889, 16.
66. NJAG Report for 1893, 26.
67. NJAG Report for 1884, 6; NJAG Report for 1885, 30–31; NJAG Report for 1888, 3, 20.
68. Telephone interview with Robert H. Bossett by author, June 27, 2006.
69. Oral history interview with Thomas H. Branch, November 8, 2002, by Michelle Carrera, New Jersey National Guard Militia Museum collection, Sea Girt.
70. Scott S. Sheads and Anna von Lunz, "The Rodman, Queen of the Smoothbore Cannons," *Cultural Resources Magazine* 20, no. 14 (1997), Cultural Resources, National Park Service, U.S. Department of the Interior, Washington, D.C.
71. Ibid.
72. NJAG Report for 1887, 16, 76–78; NJAG Report for 1889, 8.
73. NJAG Report for 1896, 21.
74. http://www.cwartillery.org/ve/rodman.html.
75. NJAG Report for 1897, 42; NJAG Report for 1900, 16; Emanuel Raymond Lewis, *Seacoast Fortifications of the United States: An Introductory History* (Annapolis, MD: Leeward Publications, 1979), 78–89.
76. *New York Times*, August 22, 1885; *Trenton Times*, July 24, 1890; NJAG Report for 1893, 191; NJAG Report for 1896, 232.
77. *Trenton Times*, July 18, 1901; *Trenton Daily True American*, July 12, 13, 14, 15, 1904.
78. *New York Times*, July 23, 1893.
79. NJAG Report for 1894, 53; Jim Foral, "The Truth About the 1903 Palma," *Gun Digest* 2004 (Iola, WI: Krause Publications, 2003); Major General Winfield Scott Price, "Sea Girt Rifle Range: The Cradle of Modern Rifle Shooting in America," unpublished monograph in NGMMNJ Collection.
80. Lieutenant Colonel Edgar N. Bloomer, "Historical Sketch of the New Jersey National Guard," in *Historical and Pictorial Review, National Guard of the State of New Jersey* (Baton Rouge, LA: Army and Navy Publishing, 1940), xxxvii; *New York Times*, May 8, 1898. Voorhees, New Jersey state senate president, was elevated to acting governor in February 1898 when Governor John W. Griggs resigned to become United States attorney general. Voorhees later served as elected governor from 1899 to 1902.
81. *Trenton Daily True American*, July 25, 1902; *New York Times*, July 25, 1902.
82. New Jersey Quartermaster General's Report for 1902 (Trenton), 9.
83. *Newark (NJ) Sunday Call*, July 1, 1906.

Chapter 4
84. Elliston Morris to "My Dear Friend," May 28, 1896; Wall Township Tax Bill for 1898, Morris Family Papers, MCHA, Folder #1; bill for telephone installation from New York and New Jersey Telephone Company, Morris Family Papers, Folder #2; Venino, *Sea Girt*, 6.

85. Joseph Eid, *Trolleys in the Coast Cities* (privately published, 1979). Wreck Pond, then still an open inlet of the sea, had a different configuration then than it does today.
86. Sea Girt Lighthouse Citizens' Committee, "The Sea Girt Light House: Erected 1896, Decommissioned 1945, Restored, 1981–1982, Centennial 1996."
87. "Sea Girt Light House"; Russell Roberts and Rich Youmans, *Down the Jersey Shore* (New Brunswick: Rutgers University Press, 1993), 244.
88. Typescript of report dated September 19, 1907, *Morris Family Papers*, MCHA, Folder #2; *New York Times*, September 22, 1907.
89. "Sea Girt, The Summer Capital of New Jersey," 3, 8, *Morris Family Papers*, MCHA, Folder #2.
90. Ibid., 14–15.
91. Lewis Historical Publishing, *Monmouth County*, 525, 527; Venino, *Sea Girt*, 8; *Asbury Park Evening Press*, September 15, 1914; application copy in Morris Family Papers, Folder #3;Tootell, "History of Crescent Park"; Venino, *Sea Girt*, 9, 20, 34; "The Borough of Sea Girt, New Jersey," mimeographed fact sheet, circa 1961, in Sea Girt Library Collections.
92. Tootell, "History of Crescent Park"; Charles E. Emerick to Marriott C. Morris, February 20, 1919, Morris Family Papers, Folder #3; Venino, *Sea Girt*, 17–18, "Borough of Sea Girt."
93. For the story of the Harris killing and investigation, see George Joynson, *Murders in Monmouth: Capital Crimes from the Jersey Shore's Past* (Charleston, SC: The History Press, 2007), 43–49.
94. Venino, *Sea Girt*, 37; *The Stockton in the Pines*, Sea Girt New Jersey, 10–11, Morris Family Papers, Folder #3.
95. *Eau Clair Sunday Leader*, July 21, 1912; *New York Times*, July 28, 22, 1912.
96. Arthur S. Link, "Woodrow Wilson," in Paul A. Stellhorn and Michael J. Birkner, *The Governors of New Jersey, 1664–1974* (Trenton: New Jersey Historical Commission, 1982), 177–82.
97. *New York Times*, June 6, 1915.
98. Bloomer, "Historical Sketch," xxix–xxx.
99. Ibid., xxxi; Walter E. Edge, *A Jerseyman's Journal: The Autobiography of a Businessman, Governor, Diplomat* (Princeton: Princeton University Press, 1948), 100–07; Lewis Historical Publishing, *Monmouth County*, 528.
100. Unidentified newspaper clipping in Paul Micelli file, NGMMNJ; *New York Times*, August 25, 1919.
101. *Trenton Evening Times*, May 13, 1920; unidentified newspaper clipping dated May 15 [1920] in NGMMNJ collection; *Newark Sunday Call*, June 13, 1920.
102. Unidentified newspaper clipping dated July 17 [1920], NGMMNJ collection; *Elizabeth Times*, July 28, 1920; *Philadelphia Evening Public Ledger*, July 30, 1920. The Tremont later became a beachfront bar. It was eventually torn down and replaced by housing. Shultz, "Sea Girt"; unidentified newspaper clipping in Paul Micelli file, NGMMNJ collection. Micelli staged summer demonstration flights at Sea Girt throughout the 1920s, including performances on Governor Moore's annual Crippled Kiddies Day. He survived another crash, in 1929 at Beach Haven, which killed three passengers, and lived to die in bed of unknown causes. *New York Times*, July 1, 1929; August 24, 1927.
103. *New York Times*, January 19, 1921; copy of recruiting flier in NGMMNJ collection; unidentified newspaper clipping dated May 29, 1921, in NGMMNJ Collection.
104. *Elizabeth Daily Journal*, July 13, 19, 1921.
105. *Trenton Evening Times*, July 23, 1921; *Newark News*, June 13, 1921.
106. Steven Hart, *The Last Three Miles: Politics, Murder and the Construction of America's First Superhighway* (New York: The New Press, 2007), 38–40.
107. Fleming, *New Jersey*, 174–77; Richard J. Connors, *A Circle of Power: The Career of Jersey City Mayor Frank Hague* (Metuchen, NJ: Scarecrow Press, 1971), 12, 32–35. Hague was never directly elected as mayor by the voters. Jersey City had a commission form of government and he was elected a commissioner and then, in turn, named mayor by a majority of his fellow commissioners.
108. Warren Sickle, "Edward I. Edwards," in Stellhorn and Birkner, *Governors of New Jersey*, 190–201. Interestingly, although they accurately represented their constituencies, Edwards himself was a non-drinker, and Frank Hague neither drank nor smoked.
109. *New York Times*, August 23, 25, 1928.

110. *Burlington [Iowa] Daily Times*, August 25, 1928; *Kingsport, Tennessee Times*, August 26, 1928; *Syracuse [New York] Herald*, August 26, 28, 1928; *Newark Sunday Call*, August 26, 1928.
111. Unidentified newspaper clipping in Paul Micelli file, NGMMNJ; *New York Times*, August 26, 1928. A "wet" was an anti-Prohibitionist.
112. *Newark Sunday Call*, August 26, 1928; Clement Alexander Price, "Morgan F. Larson," in Stellhorn and Birkner, *Governors of New Jersey*, 203; Fleming, *New Jersey*, 182.f
113. Hart, *Last Three Miles*, 133; *Newark Sunday Call*, August 26, 1928.
114. Clement Alexander Price, "Morgan F. Larson," in Stellhorn and Birkner, *Governors of New Jersey*, 201–04; *New York Times*, June 12, August 28, 1932; George W. Robinson, "Governor's Cottage…Rich in Memories," *Trenton Evening Times*, October 7, 1968; Fleming, *New Jersey*, 184.
115. Fleming, *New Jersey*, 190.
116. Brian Hicks, *When the Dancing Stopped: The Real Story of the* Morro Castle *Disaster and its Deadly Wake* (New York: Free Press, 2006), 105–06, 289. The origins of the Morro Castle fire remain murky to this day. Rogers, initially considered a hero of the disaster, proved to be a man with a dubious past and a probable sociopath later jailed for attempted murder who died in prison after being convicted of a double murder. He has been cited by conspiracy buffs as an arsonist who set the blaze, and even poisoned Captain Wilmott. There is no evidence to buttress those allegations, although he was certainly capable of such acts.
117. *New York Times*, September 9, 1934; *Lowell [Massachusetts] Sun*, September 8, 1934. Technically, the men of the First Separate Battalion were New Jersey militiamen, not National Guardsmen. Their unit, formed in 1930, was not formally recognized by the federal government until September 17, 1940, when the unit became the first battalion of the 372nd Infantry Regiment. The battalion's companies were located in Newark, Trenton, Camden and Atlantic City. Colonel (retired) Len Luzky, "NJ Afro-American Militia and National Guard," unpublished monograph, NGMMNJ Collections; e-mail correspondence with Bill Dunn, trustee, Sea Girt Lighthouse, January 29, 2008; interview with Jack Geiger, February 19, 2008.
118. E-mail from Bill Dunn; *Reno [Nevada] Evening Gazette*, September 8, 1934.
119. *Galveston Daily News*, September 9, 1934; *Charleston [West Virginia] Daily Mail*, September 8, 1934; *North Adams [Massachusetts] Transcript*, September 8, 1934; *Asbury Park Press*, September 8, 1974.
120. Interview with Betty Geiger, née Farrell, February 19, 2008; *Syracuse Herald*, September 9, 1934; *Waterloo [Iowa] Daily Courier*, September 10, 1934; *San Antonio Express*, September 11, 1934; *Oakland [California] Tribune*, September 10, 1934.
121. Hicks, *When the Dancing Stopped*, 164, 181, 187, 210–12. A copy of Senate Bill 1874 is on display as part of the *Morro Castle* exhibit in the Sea Girt Lighthouse Museum.
122. Paul A. Stellhorn, "Harold G. Hoffman," in Stellhorn and Birkner, *Governors of New Jersey*, 205–09.
123. Ibid.
124. *Anniston [Alabama] Daily Star*, August 13, 1935; *Chester [Pennsylvania] Times*, July 6, 1937; Valparaiso, *Indiana Vidette Messenger*, July 6, 1937; interview with Betty Geiger; Robinson, "Governor's Cottage."
125. *Dunkirk [New York] Evening Observer*, July 10, 1935; invitation to Governor's Day, July 17, 1930, personal notes, September 18 and November 12 and telegram of December 29, 1930, all from Harold G. Hoffman to William A. Hill, courtesy Ted Hill. Governor Moore, a pioneer in recognizing and assisting people with disabilities, established the Crippled Kiddies Day as an annual event during his Sea Girt summers, and his successors continued the practice until the summer of 1941. Moore was instrumental in providing state funding for a school specifically designed for children with special needs, which he dedicated in Jersey City in September 1931. The school still exists and is currently affiliated with the Jersey City State University Special Education program.
126. Author interview with Jack Hendrickson, December 5, 2005.

Chapter 5
127. John K. Mahon, *History of the Militia and the National Guard* (New York: MacMillan, 1983), 179–80.
128. Historical and Pictorial Review, *National Guard of the State of New Jersey*, 1940, 35, ii.
129. Edward S. Shapiro, "Charles Edison," in Stellhorn and Birkner, *Governors of New Jersey*, 210–13.
130. *New York Times*, August 25, 1940.

131. Ibid; Shapiro, "Charles Edison"; Duane Lockard, *The New Jersey Governor: A Study in Political Power* (Princeton: D. Van Nostrand, 1964), 117.
132. *Frederick [Maryland] Post*, July 12, 1941; State of New Jersey, Report of Senate Investigating Committee on its Inquiry into the Cost and Methods of Subsistence Purchases at the Governor's Cottage, at Sea Girt, New Jersey, during the Summer of 1941 (Trenton, 1942) 16–17; *New York Times*, July 7, 13, 1941, April 18, 1942, August 6, 1941
133. George Raynor Thompson, Dixie R. Harris, Pauline M. Oakes and Dulany Terrett, *United States Army in World War II: The Technical Services, The Signal Corps: The Test (December 1941 to July 1943)* (Washington: Department of the Army, 1957), 52.
134. Interview with Samuel Kaye, January 22, 2008; Nat Brooks and Terry Hughes, "We Remember: The Young Ladies' View From the Home-front," *Sawbuck Gazette*, February 2006, 5–6.
135. Charles A. Edison to Stephen H. Barlow, February 19, 1942, NGMMNJ Collection; State of New Jersey, Report of Senate Investigating Committee on its Inquiry, 7; "Statement of Account—Governor's Cottage, Sea Girt, N.J.—Season 1941," NGMMNJ Collection; interview with Barbara Borab, January 26, 2008.
136. State of New Jersey, Report of Senate Investigating Committee, 8, 12, 10, 13, 21–24; Steven Gdula, *The Warmest Room in the House: How the Kitchen Became the Heart of the Twentieth-Century American Home* (New York: Bloomsbury, 2008), 47–49; Steve Striffler, *Chicken: The Dangerous Transformation of America's Favorite Food* (New Haven: Yale University Press, 2005), 16; *New York Times*, August 1, 1941.
137. *New York Times*, May 1, 1942; "Statement by James I. Bowers, Adjutant General of New Jersey, Brigadier General, NJNG," NGMMNJ Collection.
138. *New York Times*, June 28, 1942.
139. "[New Jersey] Governors' War Cabinet Minutes, 1942–1944," June 9, 2–3; July 7, 2; July 14, 1. http://www.nj.gov/state/darm/links/guides/szwaa001.html.
140. Captain George A. Rigely, "The History of the 113th Infantry Regiment," undated [1944?] monograph in NGMMNJ Collection.
141. Sea Girt Lighthouse Citizens' Committee, "The Sea Girt Lighthouse"; Dennis L. Noble, *The U.S. Coast Guard in World War II: The Beach Patrol and Corsair Fleet* (Washington, D.C.: Coast Guard Historian's Office, 1992), 8–15.
142. Robert Kurson, *Shadow Divers* (New York: Random House, 2004), 235; Brooks and Hughes, "We Remember"; interview with Allen Atheras, February 23, 2008; "Governor's War Cabinet Minutes," June 23, 1–2.
143. Obituary in *Newark News*, May 11, 1943, Sea Girt Lighthouse Collection; Marc Mappen, *Jerseyana* (New Brunswick: Rutgers University Press, 1992), 213.
144. Lurie and Mappen, eds., *Encyclopedia of New Jersey*, 888; Richard G. Fernicola, MD, *Twelve Days of Terror: A Definitive Investigation of the 1916 New Jersey Shark Attacks* (Guilford, CT: The Lyons Press, 2001), 15–22.
145. Fernicola, *Twelve Days of Terror*, 260–65; *New York Times*, August 22, 1960.
146. *New York Times*, August 26, 1960; Edward Marriott, "Savage Shore," in Nathaniel May, ed., *Shark: Stories of Life and Death from the World's Most Dangerous Waters* (New York: Thunder's Mouth Press, 2002), 38; *New York Times*, May 21, 1961.
147. Venino, *Sea Girt*, 36–40; interview with Jack Geiger, February 19, 2008.
148. Shultz, "Sea Girt"; interview with Jack Geiger, February 19, 2008; interview with Peter Anderson, February 15, 2008.
149. Report of Board of Officers Convened by Special Orders Number 154, Department of Defense, State of New Jersey Dated 23 August 1966, NGMMNJ Collection; *Manasquan Coast Star*, March 25, 1971; "Festive Farewell Planned for Governor's Mansion," unidentified undated (but probably March 1971) newspaper clipping in Sea Girt Library Collections.
150. Report of Board of Officers.
151. Ibid., appendix II; "The Governor's Mansion, Sea Girt, N.J.," unpublished monograph in NGMMNJ Collection; Robinson, "Governor's Cottage"; interview with Brigadier General (retired) Jeffrey Pierson, March 17, 2008.

152. *Asbury Park Press*, October 12, 1966; *Newark Sunday News*, April 9, 1967; John A. Kervick to Major General James F. Cantwell, June 22, 1967, NGMMNJ Collection; *Newark Evening News*, April 3, 1969. The *Newark News* ceased publication on August 31, 1972.
153. *Newark Sunday News*, October 25, 1970; *Manasquan Coast Star*, March 25, 1971; *Asbury Park Press*, May 26, 1971.
154. *Newark Star Ledger*, March 18, 1971.
155. "The Sea Girt Lighthouse"; interview with Peter Anderson, February 15, 2008.
156. Lurie and Mappen, eds., *Encyclopedia of New Jersey*, 284; Samuel Armstrong, "The State Camp Grounds," unpublished monograph, dated 1928, in NGMMNJ Collection; interview with Fred Burns, February 19, 2008.
157. Steele Mabon Kennedy, ed., *The New Jersey Almanac, 1964–1965; Tercentenary Edition* (Upper Montclair, NJ: The New Jersey Almanac, Inc.), 161; Lurie and Mappen, eds., *Encyclopedia of New Jersey*, 729; photos in collection of NGMMNJ.
158. *New York Times*, May 23, 2004, May 24, 2002.
159. WPA Federal Writers' Project, *New Jersey*, 683–684; Adeline Pepper, *Tours of Historic New Jersey* (New Brunswick: Rutgers University Press, 1965), 109; Robert Heide and John Gilman, *O'New Jersey* (New York: St. Martin's Griffin, 1998), 140–49; Willa Speiser, *New Jersey Getaways: The Complete Guide to Garden State Day Trips* (Morristown: New Jersey Monthly Press, 2001), 198–99.
160. Ed Johnson, "Officials Stand Guard Against Selling Sea Girt Site," *Asbury Park Press*, February 26, 2008. For contact information and hours of operation of the Lighthouse Museum and the National Guard Militia Museum of New Jersey, see appendix.